Quilt Blocks

Quilt Blocks

Fast & Easy Projects Using Interchangeable Squares

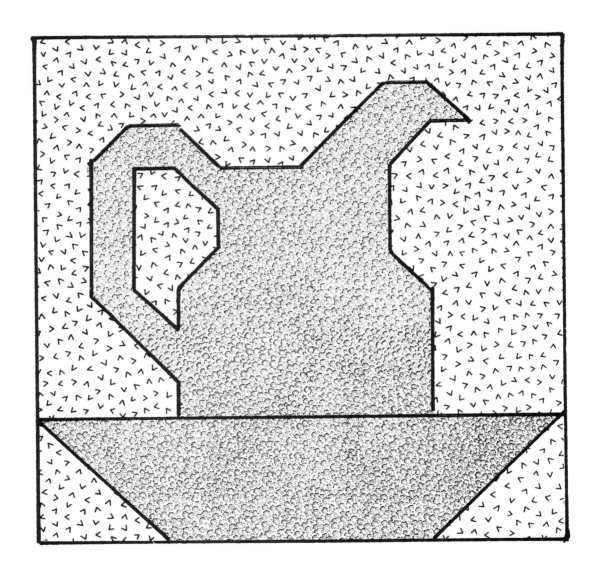

Elaine Reidy

To Phil, my kindred spirit

Curiosity found creativity hiding,
And brought it to play
On never ending paths
Of Adventure.

Library of Congress Cataloging-in-Publication Data

Reidy, Elaine.
    Quilt blocks : fast and easy projects using interchangeable
squares / Elaine Reidy.
        p.   cm.
    "A Sterling/Main Street book."
    Includes index.
    ISBN 0-8069-7423-0, — ISBN 0-8069-7422-2 (pbk.)
    1. Quilting—Patterns.   2. Patchwork—Patterns.   I. Title.
TT835.R427   1991
746.9'7—dc20   90-22427
                                            CIP

Designed by John Murphy
Typeset by Upper Case Limited, Cork, Ireland

10 9 8 7 6 5 4 3 2 1

A Sterling / Main Street Book

© 1991 by Elaine Reidy
Published by Sterling Publishing Company, Inc.
387 Park Avenue South, New York, N.Y. 10016
Distributed in Canada by Sterling Publishing
℅ Canadian Manda Group, P.O. Box 920, Station U
Toronto, Ontario, Canada M8Z 5P9
Distributed in Great Britain and Europe by Cassell PLC
Villiers House, 41/47 Strand, London WC2N 5JE, England
Distributed in Australia by Capricorn Ltd.
P.O. Box 665, Lane Cove, NSW 2066
Manufactured in the United States of America
All rights reserved

Sterling ISBN 0-8069-7423-0 trade
               0-8069-7422-2 paper

Contents

Preface

The aim of this book is to make available full-size ready-to-use patterns and instructions easy enough for the beginner and challenging enough for the advanced quilter. Most quilters appear to favor the twelve-inch block, as it is easy to handle, portable, just right for samplers, and nice for exchanging when making friendship quilts. Almost all the patterns in this book are twelve-inch blocks for these reasons. A few double-size and border patterns are included for variety. As a bonus, the six-inch pattern placement diagrams can double as a six-inch pattern, giving the quilter three modular sizes to work with for most of the blocks. Although this book is about machine quilting, all of the patterns can be used for hand methods of piecing, appliquéing, and quilting.

When I began quilting, I did not realize how addictive an activity quilting can become. Buying that "special" fabric at impulsive speed for some nebulous future project became normal predictable behavior. I have been assured by my quilting friends that this is not at all unusual. Neither is driving fifty miles out of the way in any kind of weather to attend a quilt show. Absorbing the beauty of each wonderful quilt hanging in an old musty barn on a warm spring day is a treat for the senses. There is about as great a satisfaction in looking at quilts as in making them. Each quilt is a work of art, a creation unique to the person who made it. The same pattern can be given to a hundred quilters, and, if each works independently of the other, a hundred different quilts will result. I thought about that as I chose the patterns for this book and look forward to seeing how they will be used in creative ways, how the personality of each quiltmaker will become a part of the creative process.

It is not at all unusual for me to get carried away when designing, especially if I happen to be working with a favorite image or theme. Sometimes I end up with one, two, and even three hundred variations of the same design. On the other hand, I have also spent hours and even days on *one* design. Occasionally, of course, "the well runs dry."

Color is one aspect of design which I particularly enjoy, and I expect to spend a lifetime exploring this crucial element of the craft. As an artist and quilter, color plays a major role in my everyday life. I encourage all quilters to explore the use of color, and in the following pages I suggest one way to get started in this critical dimension that is not at all inhibiting.

Quilt Blocks is a combination of designs and patterns based on experiences gathered over the years. Quilting is a medium which has provided me with much joy, an outlet which allows the creative juices to flow. Hopefully these designs will serve to stimulate your creative energy as well!

I wish to acknowledge with thanks Gloria Webster who presented a stencil workshop to my quilting group, Crossroad Quilters, and Carol Carter for sharing her knowledge on how to use waste canvas.

Elaine Reidy

Introduction
and
Instructions

Introduction and Instructions

Fabric Marking and Cutting

If you are a beginner, purchase 100 percent cotton fabric. It is easier to work with and will not stretch out of shape, pucker, and misbehave the way synthetic fabric sometimes will. If you can't find 100 percent cotton in the color you want, look for a blend with as high a percent of cotton as you can find. As you do more quilting, occasionally you might like to try a small amount of an unusual fabric for special effect.

As soon as you bring your fabric home, pre-shrink it. Do this by washing it once with a mild laundry detergent which will remove sizing and chemicals; then rinse with clear water at least twice, and dry with heat. At the same time, if you suspect that a color is not colorfast (red is often suspect), test it. Pin or baste a small piece to a slightly larger piece of white fabric, and wash in hot water and dry with heat. If the white fabric is stained red or pink, the fabric tested is not colorfast, in which case you can add ½ cup of salt to the rinse water and then put through a clear water rinse. Be sure to iron out all wrinkles in any fabric before using.

Trying to match or find just the right color fabric, especially on spur-of-the-moment buying, can be exasperating. Using pinking scissors, you can cut small swatches (about an inch square) of all the fabric you have. Staple side by side with a little space between them on plain index file cards (the kind used for filing recipes). For example, place all solid-blue and predominantly blue prints on one card. This may take a little time to do, but will be worth the frustration saved at a later date. Keep these cards in a clear plastic bag, and take them with you when you shop for fabric. If you are an impulse buyer, keep them in your pocketbook or in your car. This is your own personal fabric library that can be carried with you for easy color reference.

This is optional, but, if you intend to do a lot of quilting, it is worth the time and effort to make a *marking board*. Do this by gluing fine-grain sandpaper, gritty side up, to any firm surface, such as Masonite. This board can be portable or set up and attached in a permanent location. When you place your fabric on this marking board, the "grip" of the sandpaper will keep the fabric from slipping and sliding as you mark around the template. It will save much frustration and many a salty word.

Never use a pen to mark your fabric; you may ruin it. Use a pencil, and make the mark dark enough for you to see it. On light or white fabric, use a hard lead pencil or drafting pencil. For dark or black fabric, use a white pencil. Place the fabric *right* side up for appliqué, *wrong* side up for pieced designs. Place fabric on the marking board or working surface and mark around templates, allowing enough room visually for the ¼" seam allowance of pieced designs. Place the templates so that the arrow is parallel with the straight grain of fabric. On appliqué patterns, mark through the holes in the templates for placement of machine embroidery lines. Connect the dots to form lines on the fabric (less chance of losing them, especially on printed fabric). To cut for machine appliqué, cut right on the lines, as no seam allowance is needed.

Templates

The easiest and fastest way to make a long-lasting template that will keep its edge is to use clear plastic, thick enough to hold its shape and thin enough to cut easily. Quilt supply shops and most fabric stores carry template plastic made just for this purpose. Stencil plastic can be used as well.

To make the templates, place the clear plastic over the pattern and tape to the page with *small* pieces of masking tape so it won't move while you work. Using a black *waterproof* marking pen, trace over all the lines and mark all the information needed for each pattern piece. Arrows indicate straight grain of fabric. Be sure to mark the name of the design on *each* template so that you can return it to its proper design should it become misplaced at any time. When marking straight edges for pieced designs, it is easier to use an inking ruler than to try to mark by hand. My inking ruler is steel, with a nonskid cork layer on its underside that is indented and allows for a separation between the edge of the ruler and the surface of the plastic. You can find other styles of inking rulers in a varying price range, so shop around in stationery and art supply stores to find just the right one to fit your needs. When the marking is done, gently remove the masking tape by lifting one corner and pulling it to its opposite diagonal corner.

On patterns marked with dots to indicate placement of lines (mostly appliqué designs), use a thick needle with a sharp point, and poke a hole through each dot, using a twisting motion when the eye goes through the template. Later you will mark through these holes onto the fabric, using a sharp pencil.

Cut out the templates, using an old pair of paper scissors that are still sharp. Do not use your good fabric scissors for cutting plastic or for anything else except fabric as it will dull them. Keep the templates in an envelope with the name of the design marked on it. Many of the envelopes can be stored in empty shoe boxes, with the names of the designs marked on the outside end of the box for easy reference. The boxes stack easily for storage and do not take up a lot of space.

Machine Embroidery

To embroider is simply to outline using a zigzag satin stitch. In the appliqué designs you may need to indicate lines forming such elements as closed eyes, a mouth, and a body. Depending on the effect you want, you can zigzag with the thread closely spaced, as for satin stich, or slightly open. The lines to follow will be indicated by the pencil dot lines you marked through the template holes. Machine embroidery thread works better than regular thread as it is thinner and makes a lovely zigzag or satin stitch.

If you don't want any pencil lines or dots on your fabric, you can trace the lines to follow in pencil on white tissue paper (gift-wrap type), pin the paper to the desired location on the fabric, and then machine embroider each design. The piece of paper should be cut a little larger than the area you are stitching. As soon as you start stitching, it will begin to stay in place. Tear off the tissue paper when all the lines are done; some of it may have come partially off. Keep a wastebasket handy to toss out the smaller pieces. The larger ones can be used again. Zigzag, satin stitch, and machine running stitch can all be machine embroidered using this tissue paper method. Use of the paper also helps to control fabric creeping and puckering and will stabilize the fabric while you work on it.

To embroider thinner lines, such as cat whiskers, use a thinner stitch such as a machine running stitch. It looks best if done before the lock is formed into a quilt with backing and batting as it will remain on the surface of the fabric and look more realistic.

Somewhere on your quilt, you should mark your name, the date you finished the quilt, and any other information desired. Plan ahead and do it before the quilt "sandwich" is made. You can hand embroider the letters in a stem stitch or a running stitch if the letters are small. You might also like the very attractive look of cross-stitch embroidery, using waste canvas. When the name is completed, the waste canvas is made wet, the starch making the canvas stiff dissolves, and the threads of canvas can then be pulled off using a pair of tweezers. Only the cross-stitch name remains, looking beautiful, neat, and professional. You might consider framing the name with a line of cross-stitch or a border design around it. The colors of the embroidery thread can match and/or contrast with the colors of the quilt. Waste canvas is available in most fabric stores and comes with directions for use.

Machine Appliqué

You might want to cut the background block 1" larger all around than the finished size will eventually be. After all the appliqué and embroidery are done, iron and trim the excess to the desired size you want the block to be. As appliqué and embroidery tend to shrink the size of the block, this method will provide accuracy for piecing one block to another.

Placement of the design on the block is very important; for example, when placing an animal in profile, leave a little "breathing space" in front of its face. It is better that the tail be close to the edge of the block than the face. You want the creature to look as though it is gazing across the quilt, and not nose-to-nose with a sash. Take the time to make a pleasing arrangement of the design with good spacing.

First Method

Pin and *thoroughly baste* each piece of fabric in its permanent position exactly as you want it to look when finishing, leaving a slight space the width of two threads so that when you stitch over the raw edges of the fabric there will be room for the stitches between the shapes. If you don't leave this space, some fabrics will buckle on the edge where you are stitching, forming an unsightly ridge. Use white tissue paper between the fabric and the feed plate of your machine, and zigzag all raw edges, using a color to match the fabric to be appliquéd. Occasionally, you might use a contrasting color for a decorative effect. The zigzag can be a little open, or closed like a satin stitch. This is a personal preference. If your machine has them, you can try other edging stitches as well, making your edging stitch as wide as you need it to cover all the raw edges. Lift the presser foot *with the needle in the fabric* to change directions and to follow curves. Take the time to do a neat job of it. If you are new at it, practice first on scrap fabric before working on the block.

The loose thread, starting and ending, can be cut off where it is, or the top thread can be pulled to the back of the block and cut off there. To do this, pull the bottom thread; you will see a loop pop up. That's the top thread. With a pin or needle point inserted in the loop, pull it to the back.

On some designs, small shapes will fit on top of others, forming layers. If you wish to lighten the thickness, you can cut away the back layer that is underneath and doesn't show after the zigzag is done so you can see where to cut. Use a pair of small sharp-pointed scissors, and just be careful not to cut the layer that is underneath where you are working. This also takes care of any dark fabric or print showing through a light or white fabric on top of it. At the same time it makes the layers thinner for quilting. With machine quilting this doesn't matter as much as with hand quilting, but it makes the weight of the finished quilt lighter as well, so it is worth doing.

Second Method

Machine appliqué can also be done without basting. The fabric shapes are pressed with a hot iron on the desired background location, using any of the name-brand fusible transfer webs. Follow the directions that come with it, and then use whatever edging stitch you wish as the fabric will be perfectly flat, stuck to its backing, and *will not move* as you stitch. Always test a small piece of the fabric you intend to use before you appliqué it to the block if it is a special fabric like metallic or thin fabrics as they sometimes require that you use a pressing cloth between the fabric and the iron. Some fabrics melt and shrink when they are exposed to too much heat. Also use a single-thickness plain-white paper napkin between the fusible transfer web and your iron to take up and absorb any excess glue that may ease out of the edges. This does not happen with every name brand, but you may find it useful when it does. The paper napkin will not scorch, and the excess glue will stick to the paper and not your iron.

This method of appliqué is excellent for areas where you want to add tiny pieces of color and don't want stitches to show.

Piecing

Before you begin piecing anything, be sure the tension on your machine is correct or your entire quilt will be off. At this point you don't want any pulling and puckering from stitches that are too tight.

Piecing depends to a large extent on color. For example, a large area can be one color or broken up into several colors. Each requires a different piecing arrangement and different templates. The piecing diagrams and patterns given in this book are for the arrangements and colors shown. If you want to change the position of a color, you may

have to change the template as well. You can of course use them just as they are in any color combination you like.

For the sake of beginners, an effort was made when designing the diagrams and patterns to avoid "set-in" piecing. Therefore, the piecing is easy to do. Almost all the designs have straight seams, and only a few have a small amount of curves. If you *hand* piece the curves, you will have more control. I usually start at the fat end and work toward the narrow or pointed end. Some quilters do the reverse, so I guess it just is a matter of what works for you. If the fabric puckers on a sharp curve, you can clip the seam perpendicular and *almost to* the seam line. It should then lie flat when it is pressed.

On all seams, place the right sides together, pin, *baste,* and stitch together, using your pencil line as a guide for stitching. If you baste just under or just over the stitching line, it will be easier to remove the basting stitches later. Some quilters can just pin and stitch. I just can't seem to do it without my beginnings and endings running off the seam. It is important in piecing that the stitching is accurate so that junctions in seams will line up. Iron the seams flat open. Sew all the pieces into sections, using the diagrams as a guide, and then sew all the sections together to complete the block. On some diagrams, arrows will indicate where the sections are joined.

Sashes and Borders

If you are going to use sashes and borders, they must be planned for ahead of time. You will need to know what sash and border goes with what block for each block unit. You can also join and quilt the blocks in rows. The easiest way to plan for either is to use graph paper. Following the little squares on graph paper, draw in pencil a diagram of how many blocks you want to make, and include the sashes and borders. In the diagrams that follow, sashes are indicated by dots.

a

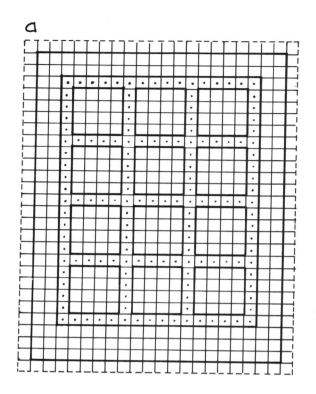

b

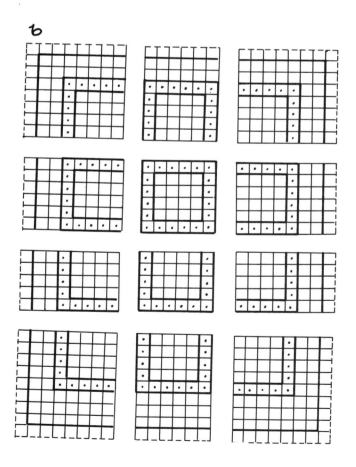

14

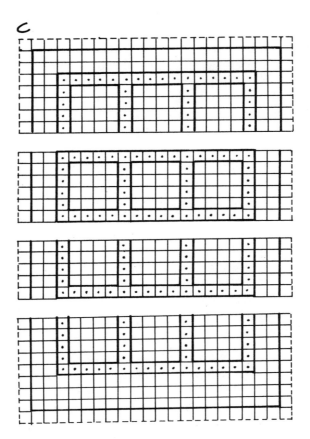

Make *two* graph paper diagrams. Keep one for reference as to how the quilt will look when finished *(a)* and a second to cut up for sash and border reference for block units or rows *(b or c)*.

Using paper scissors, cut this second diagram up into small block units, and glue or tape them to a plain piece of paper, with a space between each unit, so that you can see at a glance what sash and border goes with what block. Add about 2" extra to the outside edge of the border (indicated by the broken line in the diagram) if you want to turn the final edge to the back of the quilt; eliminate if you use continuous bias binding. You can use this method for any amount of blocks and arrange them as desired. Your block is 12", so figure sash and border size from that, using each small square on the graph paper as a guide.

For all double-size blocks, you need to make an adjustment for size *if you use sashes.* It is easy to do; just add the sash *width* to the top of the block, or divide the amount between the top and the bottom. This makes up for the "missing" sash in the middle of the double size block that would be there if it were two single 12" blocks. If you are not using sashes, the 12" by 24" block will fit with all the other 12" blocks just as they are.

Cut the sashes and borders on the grain, using a ¼" seam allowance. Pin, baste, and stitch the appropriate sashes and borders to their blocks, following your diagram. When this is done you are ready to make each block unit, or row, into a quilt sandwich.

Combine the quilt sandwich layers in this order: backing on the bottom, wrong side up; batting on top of the backing, cut to fit; quilt top over batting. Be sure to purchase *bonded* batting so flecks of batting won't come through the top later and ruin all your work. Batting comes in many thicknesses; the thicker the batting, the puffier the quilt. Thickness is a matter of personal preference.

Machine Quilting

The three layers *must be basted together* to

keep from shifting as you quilt. Use *short* stitches on top so your presser foot on your machine won't catch in them. First pin and baste *on the seam line* all around the outside edge of the block unit. This keeps your seams where they should be, not allowing them to shift when you are quilting. Then baste ³/₄" to 1" inside the seam line, using a bright red or a contrasting color and value thread. You want this line of basting to be very noticeable. Think of it as your WARNING LINE that is not to be crossed when quilting. This ³/₄" to 1" of space will give you enough room to join block unit seams later. Baste the layers together in a grid, vertically and horizontally. Start in the center each time, and work toward the outside edge. Now you are ready for the fun part – quilting!

This method of quilting a small block unit or row (then joining later) is known as "quilt-as-you-go." Use an even feed foot (also known as a walking foot), if you have one, for beautiful, trouble-free quilting. If you can't find one to fit your machine, adjust the weight of the presser foot to be lighter. On most sewing machines, this adjustment is on the top-left part, but check the manual supplied with your machine to be sure. If you have thoroughly basted, you should not have any problems.

The right side of the presser foot makes a nice gauge to follow when quilting around a design. To change directions, or to turn corners, leave the needle *in the fabric,* lift the presser foot, and continue to quilt. Remember to always stop at the WARNING LINE. Any unfinished quilting can be completed after the seams are joined and finished off, top and bottom.

If you are working in block units, *quilt about the same amount in each block.* Too much quilting in one block will change its size. If you want close background quilting with horizontal and/or vertical lines, use masking tape on the fabric as a guide by just stitching alongside the edge, using a zipper presser foot or an even feed foot. Don't leave the tape on the fabric for long periods of time because some of the residue of the tape may adhere to the fabric, especially if exposed to heat or sunshine. If this should happen, there are several ways quilters have used to get rid of the residue. Always test on scrap fabric first. One way is to rub an ice cube gently on the area; another is to place a squirt of lighter fluid on a clean white cloth and rub gently; and a third is to gently rub full-strength any type of hair shampoo in place of the lighter fluid. With any method you will then have to wash, rinse, and dry the block unit. No doubt you will find that it is much easier to remove the masking tape as soon as possible.

Transferring the Quilting Image to the Fabric
Place ordinary white tissue paper over the image or design that you want to quilt. Attach the paper with small pieces of masking tape. Using a pencil, trace the design onto the paper. Carefully remove the tape. Pin the paper to the desired location on the fabric where you want to quilt. Machine quilt in a running stitch spaced to your liking. Quilt directly on the pencil lines of the tissue paper. When all the quilting is done, remove the paper. It will tear off quite easily. The result will be wonderfully clean, pencil-free quilting.

Any appliqué pattern can double as a quilting pattern. Images that appeal to you from just about any source can be used as a line drawing for quilting. This transfer method gives you a world of images to choose from.

When you quilt by machine, the thread ends should disappear as neatly as when quilting by hand. Leave a long enough thread when starting and stopping to thread an ordinary hand sewing needle. Pull the top thread to the bottom side. You can do each individually or thread both on the needle at the same time. Take a tiny back stitch, and, very close to it, go back into the batting layer to about an inch from where you entered. Bring the needle out there to the top of the fabric. Pull the thread taut and snip off as close to the surface of the fabric as you can, being careful not to cut the fabric. The 1" "tail" of thread will remain secure between the layers and neatly out of sight.

When starting and stopping in the same place, as with a circle or a closed shape, make the beginning threads disappear when you've stitched about halfway around. Then continue to quilt until you reach the starting place, at which point you will only have the two ending threads to deal with rather than the four. This will also insure that you don't run over the beginning threads by mistake when ending. If it is a *small* closed shape, you can just pull the top thread to the back, reach under, and move the two beginning threads out of the way. With a little practice, you will find what works best for you .

Another method is to machine back stitch, and just cut off the threads to start and stop. This is of course much faster, but some quilters don't consider it as neat. The choice is yours.

Quilt each block unit, or row, and set it aside to join later. Think about how your quilting stitches can enhance the design whenever you are quilting. Quilt design templates can be purchased at fabric stores and quilt supply shops, or you can make your own.

Joining Block Units and Rows

Following your graph paper diagram, join the block units in rows on the shortest (usually horizontal) side. Join the rows together. If you're using sashes, an easy way to line them up one row on top of another is to place a ruler or straightedge vertically on the edge of the block and sash of the top row, and extend it over the horizontal sash under it. Make a small pencil mark on the horizontal sash, on the edge of the seam allowance where it won't show. Do this on each side of the vertical sashes. When you line up the horizontal sash with the next row of block units below it, each pencil mark will be a guide to line up the sashes exactly. They will be perfect.

To join the seams, pin the batting out of the way onto the backing. Pin, baste, and stitch, right sides together, the top seams first. Trim away any unwanted batting until the batting from both blocks butt together and lay flat. It is sometimes recommended here, especially if it is a long seam, to hand baste a generous zigzag stitch, joining the two batting edges together. In a small area this is not necessary. Allow one side of the fabric to lay flat. Turn the remaining side under $\frac{1}{4}$" on top of the first side. Pin and blind stitch in place. Do all the seams in this way. For uniformity, be sure the last side to be stitched in place is the same one on the top each time.

When the block units and rows are all joined, you need only turn the remaining raw edge of the border to the back and blind stitch in place. You allowed an extra two inches for this turn back earlier when making the graph diagrams. You can of course bias bind the edge instead, in which case you will not need the turn back allowance.

An alternative to this method of joining is to add the border on at the end. If you decide to do this, plan for it ahead when making the graph paper diagrams, and add the border on as though it were another row. Decorative borders are often added last, in just this way.

Your beautiful quilt is now finished unless you want to hang it on a wall, or in a quilt show, in which case you will need to make a sleeve and attach it to the back of the quilt.

Making a Sleeve

The sleeve fabric can match the backing fabric, or not, as desired. Make it wide enough to allow the bar or rod you will be using to pass through it easily, with enough room so that it won't be tight. If it is going to hang in a show, find out if they require a definite sleeve size.

Measure the width across the top of the quilt and subtract 3" or 4" from each side. That measurement will be the length of the sleeve. Turn under the raw edges on the two ends of the sleeve the usual ¼" and iron or finger press. Turn under another ¼" to ⅝" and top stitch. Place the *wrong* sides together and stitch a seam down the length of the sleeve. Place the seam side down against the back of the quilt so that it is even, with the same amount of space showing on each end of the quilt under it. It should not be seen from the front of the quilt when it is hanging. Be sure to allow enough room so that it will not show at the top of the quilt, and leave enough "play" for the rod to slide through easily.

Blind stitch into place, both above and below the sleeve seam. Some stitches should go all the way through all the layers of the quilt, so make them small and, if possible, line them up with a seam on the front of the quilt so they won't show.

Sleeve making differs from person to person. Some quilters use tabs as well as sleeves on their quilts. Tabs are like small sleeves stitched onto the quilt at the width of the tabs rather than at the length. They are then placed at the top of the quilt where needed

for support. Tabs are often done in a matching decorative fabric because, unlike the sleeve, they show.

Continuous Bias Binding

On some quilts and projects you may want to finish off the edges with bias binding. You can use store-bought bias binding, but it won't give you the wide range of color, fabric, and size that you will have if you make your own. Continuous bias binding eliminates the many joining seams that you would have on bias strips if you made them one at a time and then had to join them to each other.

To make your own continuous bias binding, you first need to find the true bias of the fabric you are using. One way this can be done is by cutting the fabric into a perfect rectangle. If this is the first time you are making a continuous bias binding, you might want to try this on a small sample of fabric first.

I.

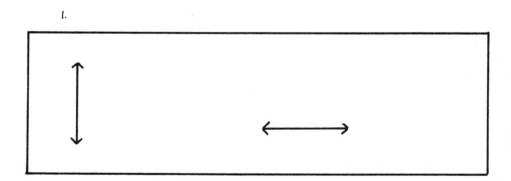

2.

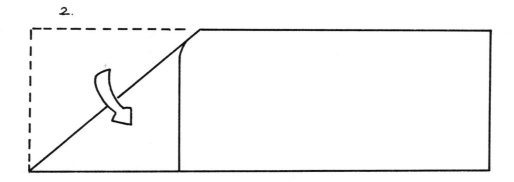

3.

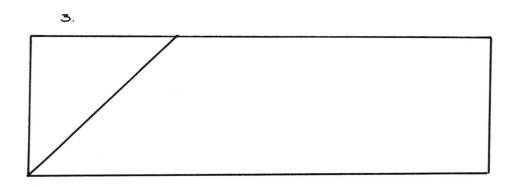

4.

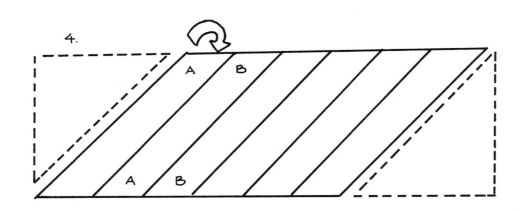

FIG 5.

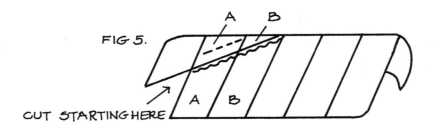

CUT STARTING HERE

Following the diagram, cut the fabric on the straight of the grain (indicated by arrows) into a large even rectangle, both sides parallel (1). Take the upper left corner and fold down until the entire left edge matches and is directly on top of the bottom edge (2). The true bias is where the crease forms an angle. Press the crease and/or mark it with a pencil. This line is the first edge of the continuous bias binding (3). Decide how wide you want the binding to be, and, using that measurement, draw parallel lines from the first one, continuing on the bias across the fabric. Cut off the unwanted fabric on the ends (dash lines), and mark the first three strips A, A and B, and B (4). Join the rectangle, forming a tube, matching A to A, and B to B. Pin, baste, and stitch this seam, and then cut *on* the diagonal line, starting at A, and continue until the end (5). The result will be one long strip of continuous bias binding. Stitch the binding to the desired edge, right sides together, and turn the remaining raw edge to the back. Blind stitch in place.

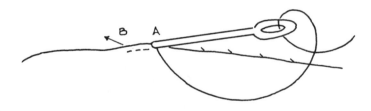

Lift up the edge that you want to blind stitch, and, about ¼" under it, take two or three small stitches. Working from right to left, bring the needle up *through the fold* of the edge to be stitched in place (A). Hold the edge in place with your left hand (thumb on fold) and push the needle *into* the fold for a short distance, about ¹⁄₁₆" to ¼" and then *out* the edge of the fold (B). The next stitch starts directly *under* the point where the thread came out of the fold. Take a tiny stitch under the fold, and come back into it, continuing a short distance as before. Repeat these steps until the edge is stitched in place. To end, take one or two tiny back stitches, and run the needle between the lay-ers of fabric where it won't show. Bring the thread out to the top of the fabric and snip off the thread close to the surface of the fabric, being careful not to cut the fabric under it.

Stenciling

Stenciling can be used in any design area that is too small or too complicated to piece or appliqué with ease. Most supplies can be found in art supply and fabric stores. There is more than one way to stencil, but you will find the following method easy to do. Water-based paints can be used as an alternative and are easy to clean up.

Supplies needed are:

Freezer paper (available at supermarkets)
Masking tape
Iron
4H or 6H pencil
Stencil knife or X-acto knife and cutting surface
Paintsticks (oil-based) in colors desired
Palette knife or small thin spatula
A stencil brush for each color (saves cleaning the brush at every color change)
Turpentine and paper towels for cleaning up

Stenciling Letters or Shapes

Cut the fabric 3" or 4" larger than needed for the area you wish to stencil. Remove any loose thread. No thread can be allowed to find its way under your fabric, or on top, as it will make unwanted lines on your stencil. The fabric can be trimmed to fit the desired size after the stencil is finished, dried, and heat set.

Cut two pieces of freezer paper about ½" smaller than the fabric. Iron one piece, *shiny side down,* on the wrong side of the fabric. (Use a wool setting, no steam.) If the paper forms small bubbles, remove it and re-press. It can be used several times, but at some point it will no longer stick.

Using the 4H or 6H pencil, trace the letters or shapes or design (centered) on the second piece of freezer paper (shiny side down). Tape the paper (use masking tape) to a cutting surface, and cut out all the letters or shapes that you want to stencil, using the stencil knife. *Save all the pieces.*

Iron the stencil on the *right* side of the fabric. Iron all the pieces back into their original position. Remove *one letter (or shape) at a time* to stencil. Remove only those pieces where you want that particular color to go.

Tape a good-size piece of freezer paper to your working surface. This is your palette. Remove the seal, if your paintstick has one, by rubbing the paintstick on the palette in a small circle until the seal is broken and enough paint is on the palette to begin the stencil process. Add paint as needed. Use the color as is, or, if you wish to mix with other colors, *rub a separate circle of color* for each color desired, and mix on an unused part of the paper, using a palette knife. Start with a *lighter* color than you think you want, and add more color as needed to darken.

Holding the stencil brush in a vertical position, tap, tap, tap it onto the color until enough paint is on the brush. Brush on the fabric surface where the first letter or shape is removed. Use a short stroke or circular tapping motion. When the area is filled with the desired color, return the freezer paper letter or shape over the color and iron it back in place. Remove the second letter or shape and continue the stencil process until all are done. Putting the letter back in place each time keeps one color from hitting the color next to it if you are using more than one color at a time.

When finished, soak a paper towel with turpentine; clean and then wash and rinse your brushes. Carefully remove all the freezer paper. You can save it to use again if desired. Allow the paint to dry at least three days. Heat set so the paint will become permanent. Use a dry iron (wool setting) directly on the fabric stencil.

Color

Color is a very personal matter. What colors to use must be the decision of the quilter, as it is with the artist who creates a work of art. Volumes of information about color interaction have been written and are in any good bookstore in the art section or in your local library. You will find that, no matter how much you know, favorite colors will find their way into your quilts, regardless of the color scheme. They are intrinsic, a part of the inner you. Be proud to use them over and over as you wish because they are as much a part of you as your signature.

Use the colors that you like to start with. If you need a change of pace now and then, and would like to invent new color combinations, try using paint swatch samples from the paint or hardware store. They are free for the asking and will give you lots of colors to experiment with. Cut between each color with paper scissors to separate them, and turn them upside down so that you can't see the colors. Mix them all up and then turn over four or five at a time, placing them close together so that you can see how the colors look together and affect one another. Do this several times. Chances are that you will find color combinations that are new to you, that you like, and never thought of using before. Match them as closely as you can to fabric that you have on hand, and bring them with you if you need to purchase a new one.

Basic Color Mixing
The *primary* colors you will use are red, yellow, and blue. The *secondary* colors you can mix if you can't find the corresponding paintsticks are orange (red + yellow), purple (red + blue), and green (yellow + blue). In-between the primary and secondary colors on the color circle are the *intermediate* colors you can mix by using a primary with a neighboring secondary color. These are yellow + green, blue + green, blue + violet, red + violet, red + orange, and yellow + orange. These are pure hue or pure color. You can modify these colors further by adding more

of one color than the other. If you add more yellow to yellow-green, for example, you will have a yellower yellow-green. If you add more green, you will have a greener yellow-green.

To change the value and intensity and modify a color even further, you can tint, tone, or shade it. A *tint* is adding white to any color. It will make the colors more pastel, lighter – the type many quilters use for baby quilts. A *tone* is adding gray (black + white) to any color. It will make the color softer, grayer – the type often used for country-style quilts. You can also use complementary colors to tone (opposites on the color wheel), but this becomes more complicated depending on whether you use the warm or cool of a particular color, and you may not get as nice a gray as with black and white. Start with more white, and add a *small* amount of black, a little at a time, until the desired value of gray is mixed. Time and experience are the only teachers here. A *shade* is adding black to any color. It will darken the color and make it more somber. Many quilters use shades of color for a mood change or to contrast with lighter colors. Start by adding a *small* amount of black, and add more as needed to get the desired color.

Even if you don't do stenciling now, you might at some point, so this information on color will be helpful when you need it. It will also be useful if you intend to dye fabric.

Pieced
Design
Blocks

Pieced Design Blocks

You will find nineteen quilterrific blocks to piece in this section. A 12" tree, wreath, angel, jam jar, pineapple, coffeepot and cup, bowl and pitcher, blue jay, coffee grinder, baby duck, hen, bird and bath, teapot, crab, cats one, two, and three; and two 12" by 24" blocks, the oil lamp and the lobster. They can be used by themselves or in any combination with other 12" blocks you may already have in your collection.

All of the blocks are pieced together in sections. The diagrams for each block are easy to follow, along with the written step-by-step individual instructions. The first diagram shows how the finished block will look; the second, how it is pieced in sections; and the third – the larger easy-to-follow 6" diagram (shown with most of the blocks) – indicates each pattern placement with its own corresponding letter. The 6" diagram can also double as another pattern for small quilts and projects on the designs that are easy to do. Each design is presented in order of difficulty – easy, moderately easy, some experience needed, and, finally, for the advanced quilter. A special effort was made to avoid "set-in" piecing to make things easier for beginners.

The pieced design blocks are illustrated to give you an idea of what they will look like in color. Yours can look the same or vastly different, depending on how you use color, fabric, and textures. The variety and suggestions for variation will give you years of pleasure and enjoyment.

Note that the $\frac{1}{3}$ yard of fabric for each block is measured as you would purchase fabric by the yard . One-third yard would be 12" of your choice of fabric no matter what its width. You would have leftover fabric. Another way to estimate the fabric needed is just to consider it 12" by 12" or 12" by 24" of scrap fabric for each block. The $\frac{1}{3}$ yard estimate is given for each block in this book. Add $\frac{1}{4}$" seam allowance.

1.
Christmas Tree

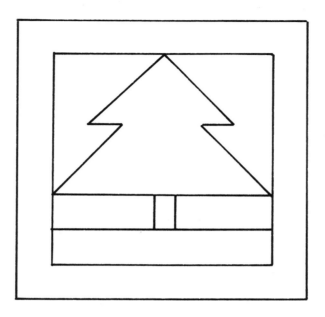

The 12" Christmas Tree block is very easy to do and requires only eight pattern pieces, A-H. All pattern pieces are actual size. Approximately 1/3 yard (30.5 cm) of solid color cotton fabric is called for. Snowflakes are added by using fabric paint.

You can, of course, use any combination of colors that you wish. I have suggested only four – Christmas red, holly green, royal blue, and white. This tree is shown in color on page 65 and is included in the Christmas Sampler quilt project illustrated on page 113.

Assembling the Block

1. Cut all of the necessary pattern pieces adding a 1/4" seam allowance.

2. Using the illustrations and diagrams as a guide, sew the sections together in rows.

   Row 1: Starting at the top F,D,A, and D.
   Row 2: Moving down. G, B, and G.
   Row 3: E, C, and E.

Sew F to F, and add to row 3. Add the remaining H to each side. Your block is now complete.

3. The Snowflakes may now be added. The type of fabric paint I use is an acrylic water base that comes in a jar. Some brands are sold in a tube. Some need to be heat-set; some do not. Follow the manufacturer's directions. Some fabrics will require two or more coats of paint to produce a sufficiently white snowflake. Don't worry about placing the dot of white paint exactly on top of the one underneath as a slight overlap adds to the softness of the edge. Most craft shops and many fabric shops sell fabric paints.

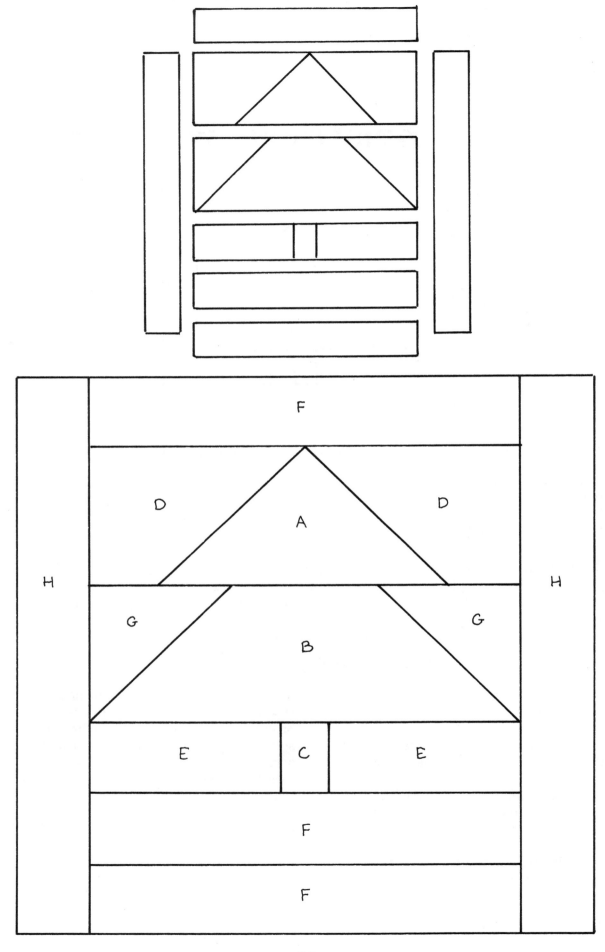

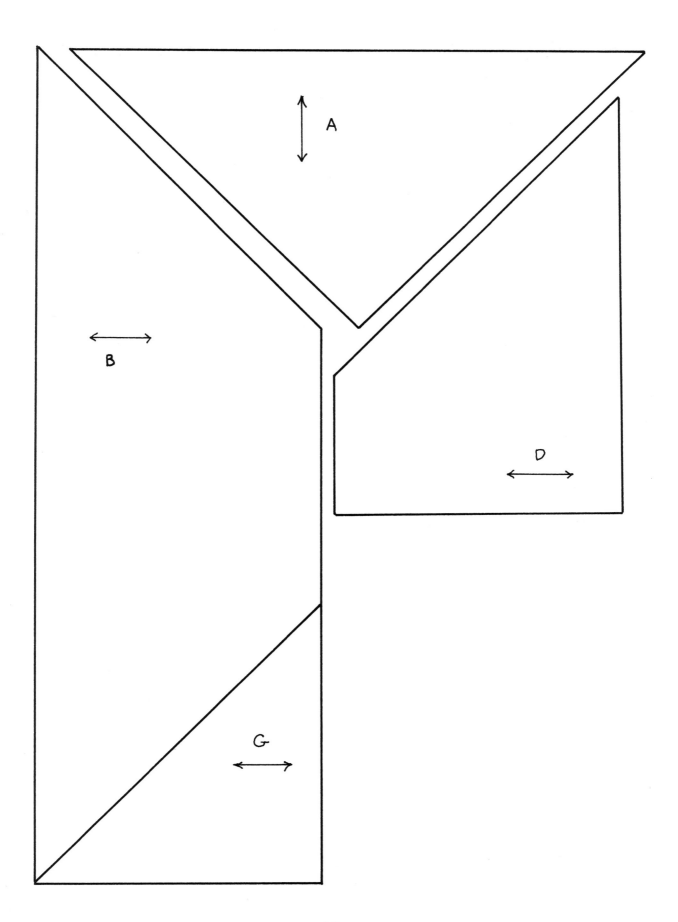

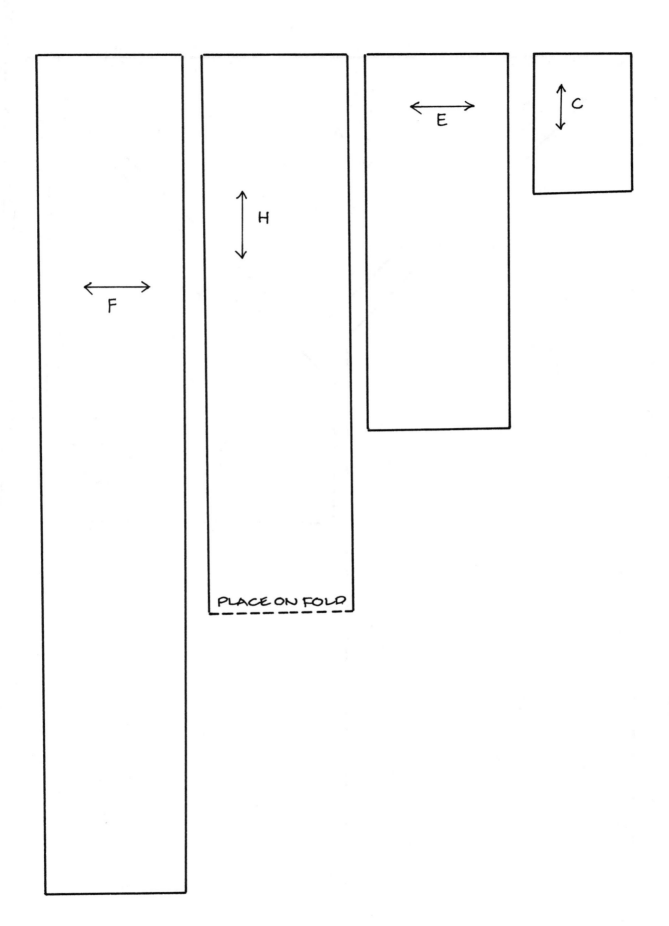

F

H

E

C

PLACE ON FOLD

2.
Christmas Wreath

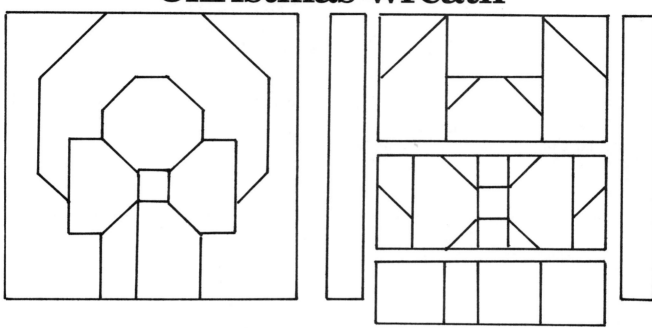

The 12" Christmas Wreath block is easy to do and requires only ten pattern pieces, A-J. All pattern pieces are actual size. About ⅓ yard (30.5 cm) of solid-color cotton fabric, plus a small additional piece of red fabric for the berries and a matching small piece of fusible transfer web for attaching the berries to the wreath, is required. There are several brands of fusible transfer web available in fabric stores. Follow the manufacturer's directions.

The colors shown here are holly green for the wreath, Christmas red for the bow and berries, and a gray red for the shadow side of the bow ribbon. A small amount of yellow fabric paint can be added to the berries for additional color. This wreath design block is shown in color on page 65 and is included in the Christmas Sampler quilt project illustrated on page 113.

Assembling the Block

1. Cut all of the necessary pattern pieces, adding a ¼" seam allowance.

2. Using the illustrations and diagrams as a guide, sew the sections together in rows.

 Row 1: Starting at the bottom. E, G, E, and E.

 Row 2: Moving up. D + D; C and C to A; B + B + B; C and C to A; D + D.

 Row 3: Top section. F + J; I + C and C to A; F + J.

Add the remaining H to each side. Your block is now complete.

Appliqué the berries, and yellow fabric

29

paint on the berries may now be added in the same manner as the snowflakes on the Christmas Tree block.

Options

The wreath can also be done with scrap green print or with scrap solid-green cotton fabric. Pattern pieces I and J can be cut once more to make additional areas for color. How you cut them is your choice. Corner to corner, making triangular shapes, is one way you might like to try.

Moiré taffeta in red or rose is a lovely alternative to cotton. It makes a very decorative bow and ribbons.

The berries could also be stenciled on the fabric, using the technique described in the Introduction and Instructions as a guide.

The 6" diagram can double as a pattern for a mini-wreath wall quilt or for potholders.

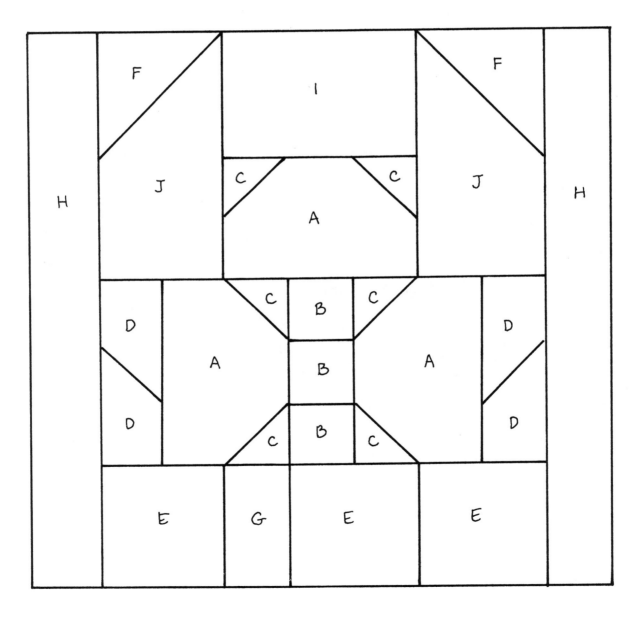

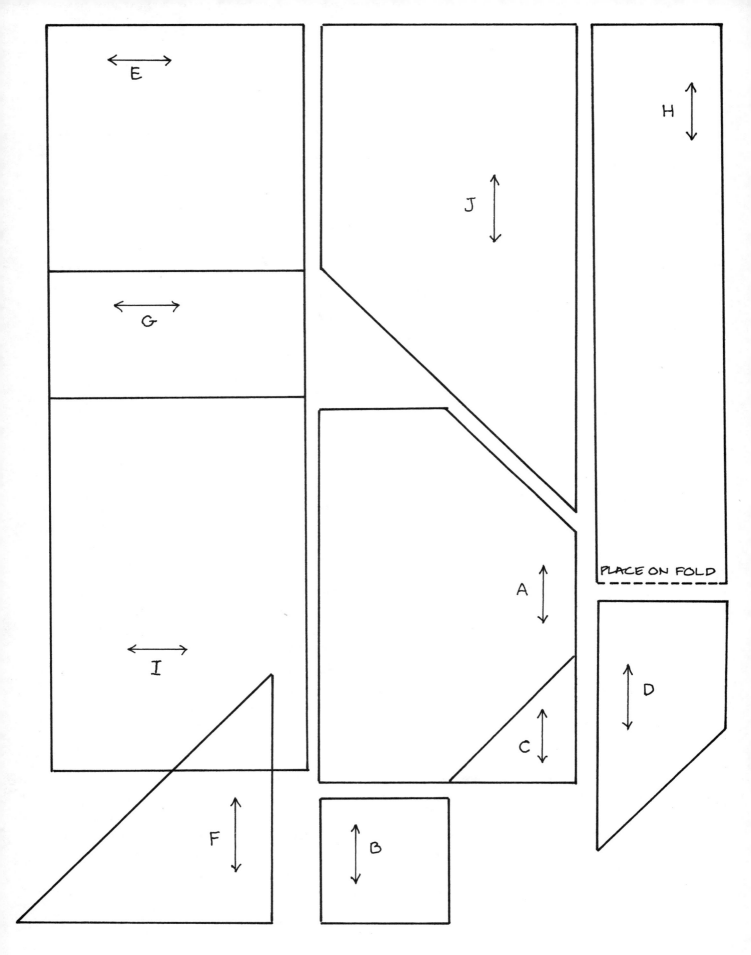

E

G

I

J

H

A

C

D

PLACE ON FOLD

F

B

31

3.

Angel

The 12" Christmas Angel block is moderately easy to do as it has some curved piecing and seventeen pattern pieces, A-O. There are two C's and two L's for the wings to enable you to distinguish the feather patterns on the wings. All pattern pieces are actual size. About 1/3 yard (30.5 cm) of solid-color cotton fabric is needed.

The wing patterns on each side are exactly the same, one side being the reverse of the other. You will therefore need to flop all of those pattern pieces except B and E. The illustrations and one wing on the diagram show how the feather pattern on the wings will look.

I advise *hand piecing* the curves, especially if you are a beginner. I find it easier to start at the "fat" end and sew toward the point. Some quilters do the opposite. Try it both ways to see which works best for you. Since the pieces are small, you should not need to clip curves. The halo pattern, piece O, is included, even though it is not shown in the diagram. The angel's hair can be any natural hair color; reddish brown is used in my example. The skin and dress color can vary as well. This Angel block is shown in color on page 66 and is included in the Christmas Sampler quilt illustrated on page 113.

Assembling the Block

1. Cut all the necessary pattern pieces, adding a ¼" seam allowance.

2. Using the illustrations and diagrams as a guide, sew the sections together in rows.

> *Row 1:* Starting at the bottom. E, A, and E.
>
> *Row 2:* Moving up. C + L-2; D + I; G and G to F; G and G to F; D + I; L 2 + C.
>
> *Row 3:* Left side. C + L-1; L + C-l; B; M + C-2.
>
> *Row 4:* Middle. N + L and N + L; I and I to J; L and L and I and I to K, I and I to J; G + H + G; G + H + G.
>
> *Row 5:* Right side. M + C-2; C + L-l; L + C; B.

Your Angel block is now complete.

3. The feather pattern may now be added onto the wings. You can do a running stitch by hand with embroidery thread or by machine with any shiny white thread that will work in your machine. Appliqué or stencil the halo over the head.

Options

The halo is beautiful when appliquéd in gold metallic fabric using a fusible transfer web. You may need to use a pressing cloth between the metallic and your iron, as some of the metallic fabrics melt and shrink when heat is applied. Test first on scrap fabric before you do the appliqué on your block. Special fabric for the angel's dress could also be with gold and/or silver thread for a "heavenly" effect.

The little angel can become a banner in a child's room. You can appliqué or stencil the child's name on the banner for a more personal touch. In like manner, quilting groups might enjoy making a banner with MY ANGEL on it for their Christmas boutique. This angel block will be a delightful addition to a child's apron, a tote bag, or on a Christmas place mat and table runner. You will think of many ways to use this design. Your little Christmas Angel will be very special.

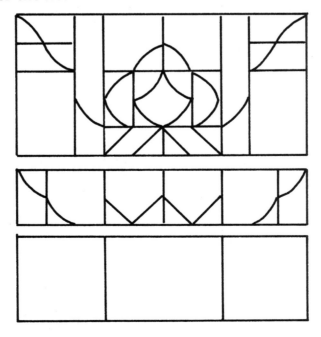

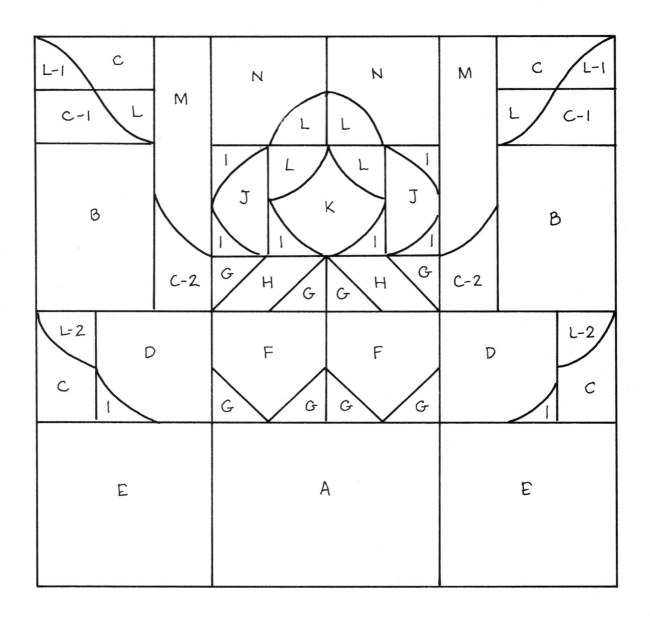

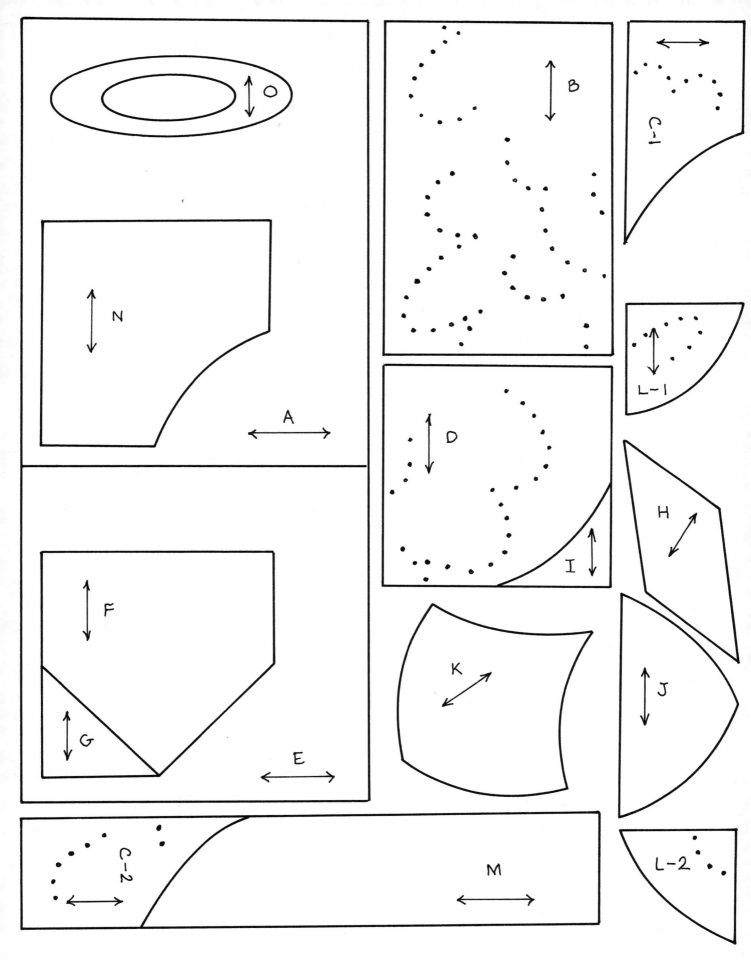

4.
Jam Jar

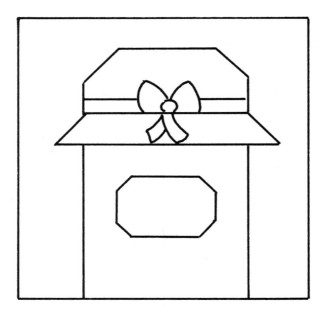

The 12" Jam Jar block is a good one for beginners as it is easy to do and has only nine pattern pieces, A-I. All pattern pieces are actual size. About ⅓ yard (30.5 cm) of solid and print fabric is needed.

If you can find a print fabric that illustrates fruit (strawberries, raspberries, grapes, etc.), your jam jar will be more realistic; otherwise, the color print will be whatever "jam" you want to make. Strawberry jam is shown in the color illustration on page 66. White fabric or off-white is advised for the jam label (pattern H), and a neutral color for the background will look good. This jam jar is also included in the Town and Country Sampler quilt design illustrated in color on page 115.

Assembling the Block

1. Cut all of the necessary pattern pieces, adding a ¼" seam allowance.

2. Using the illustrations and diagrams as a guide, sew the sections together in rows.

Row 1: Top section starting at the left side. A + C.
Row 2: Middle. C and C to D, G, B; add B.

Row 3: Right side. A + C.
Row 4: Bottom section, inside. I + I + I + I to H, add on F and F. Add on B and E. Add an E to each side.

The piecing of this block is now complete. Pattern G, indicated on the diagram by dash lines, can be eliminated.

3. To cross-stitch the letters J, A, and M on pattern H (the label), trace the

X marks onto a white piece of paper. Go over them with a black waterproof ink marking pen. Tape that piece of paper to your window in the daytime (the daylight outside the window will act as a light box, allowing you to see the letters through the fabric). Center your block over the letters until they are even on the label, then tape the block to the window, using masking tape. Mark the cross-stitch letters on your label in pencil, only dark enough to read, and then remove the block from the window. Cross-stitch the letters with two strands of embroidery thread in a color that will go well with the "jam." Your block is now complete.

Options

The ribbon (G) and bow (dash lines) can be store-bought. The ribbon top is stitched into place after the block is made, and then the bow is attached to the middle with small stitches from the back side of the block where they won't show.

Another method for including the label is to use one large pattern combining all the bottom jam portion of the design, and then to appliqué the label on top of the "jam." The letters can also be added to the label, using waste canvas (see the discussion of waste canvas in the Introduction and Instructions under the subject of machine embroidery). Waste canvas comes in several sizes and will give you guidelines to cross-stitch the letters J, A, M in place.

White eyelet cotton fabric can also be pieced for the white jar cover, and white lace added onto the bottom edge will add softness and give a decorative country touch.

The 6" piecing diagram can double as a pattern on this design to make beautiful and colorful potholders. Just bind the edges with a matching or contrasting fabric.

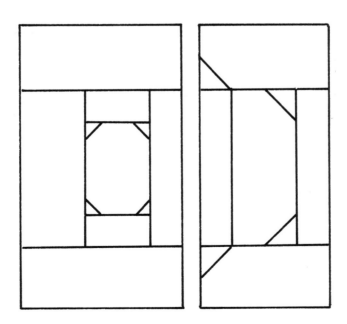

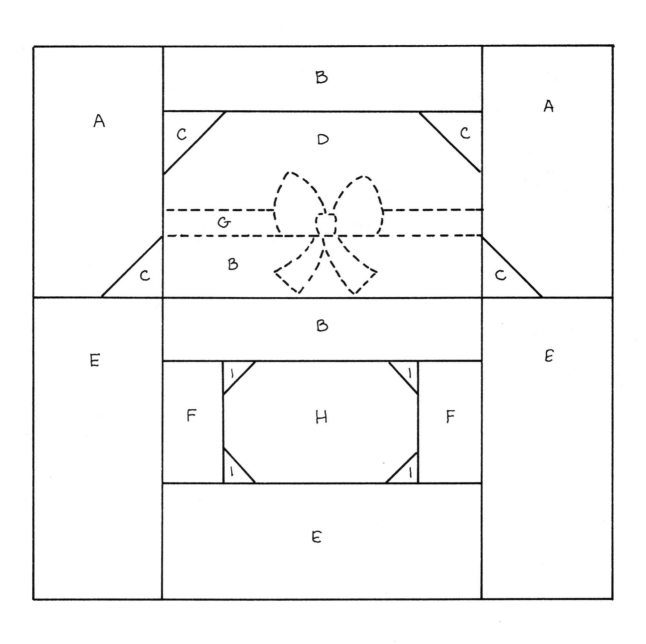

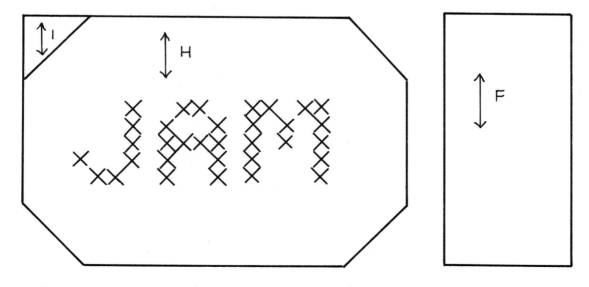

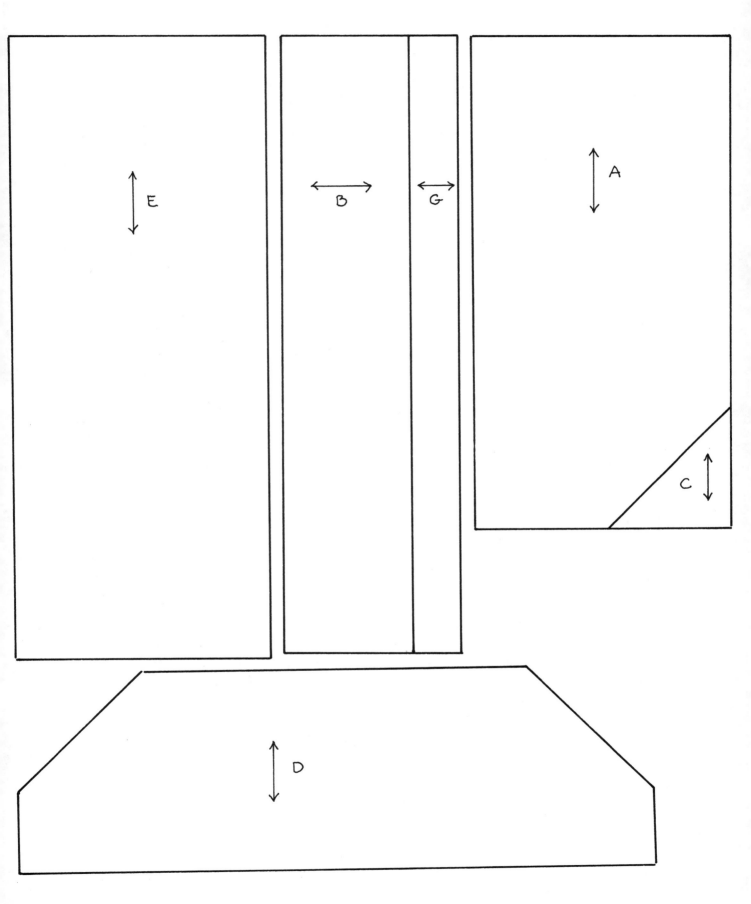

5.
Pineapple

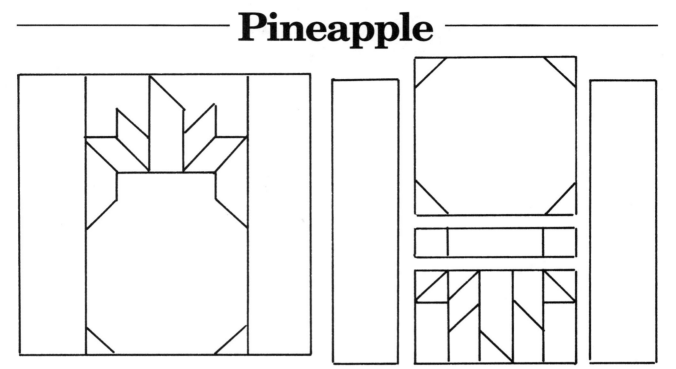

The 12" Pineapple block is very easy to do and is thus an excellent pattern for beginners. It has only nine pattern pieces, A-I. All of the pattern pieces are actual size. About ⅓ yard (30.5 cm) of print and solid fabric is needed.

The Pineapple block is good with a fabric that will imitate the natural texture and color of the fruit. Diagonal quilting to form a diamond pattern on the base of the pineapple will enhance this effect. Follow along the edge of masking tape as described in the Introduction and Instructions for machine quilting. The leaf portion gives you an opportunity to use different greens. The side panels (panel A) are other areas to add a color accent.

The pineapple is a traditional welcome sign and was used as such in early colonial times. Yours will say "welcome" in any size quilt—as a wall quilt on your door or in your dining room. This block design is shown in color on page 67 and is included in the Town and Country Sampler quilt project illustrated in color on page 115.

Assembling the Block

1. Cut all the necessary pattern pieces, adding a ¼" seam allowance.

2. Using the illustrations and diagrams as a guide, sew the sections together in rows.

Row: Bottom of middle section. C + C + C + C to H.
Row 2: Middle. I, G, I.
Row 3: Top of middle section, moving left to right. B, C, C.
Row 4: E, D, C.

40

Row 5: C, F.
Row 6: E, D, C.
Row 7: B, C, C.

Add an A to each side. Your block is now complete.

Option

For a greater challenge, you might consider making a three-dimensional leaf section and attaching it where the leaf portion joins the pineapple. The background piecing can be replaced with one template for a complementary colored fabric. The 3-D leaves can be stitched by doubling the patterns (reversing one set), placing the right sides of the fabric together, and stitching a seam all around, leaving the bottom *open* to turn right side out. Iron flat, then stitch them into the desired position next to pattern G.

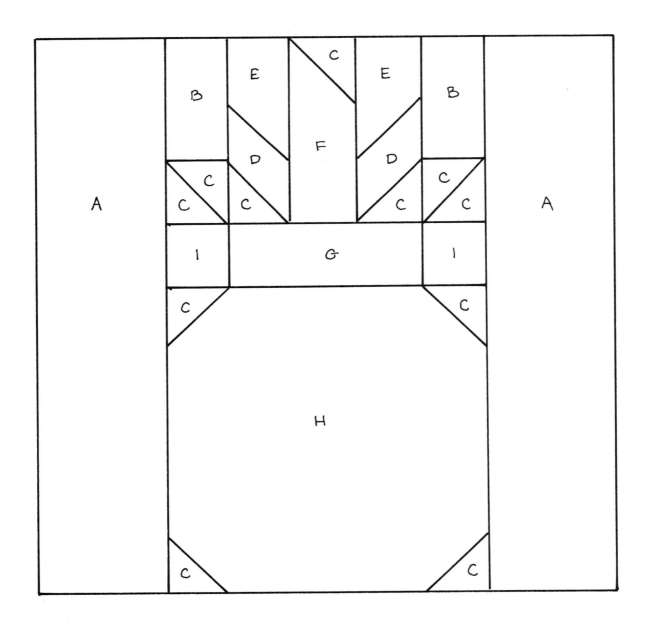

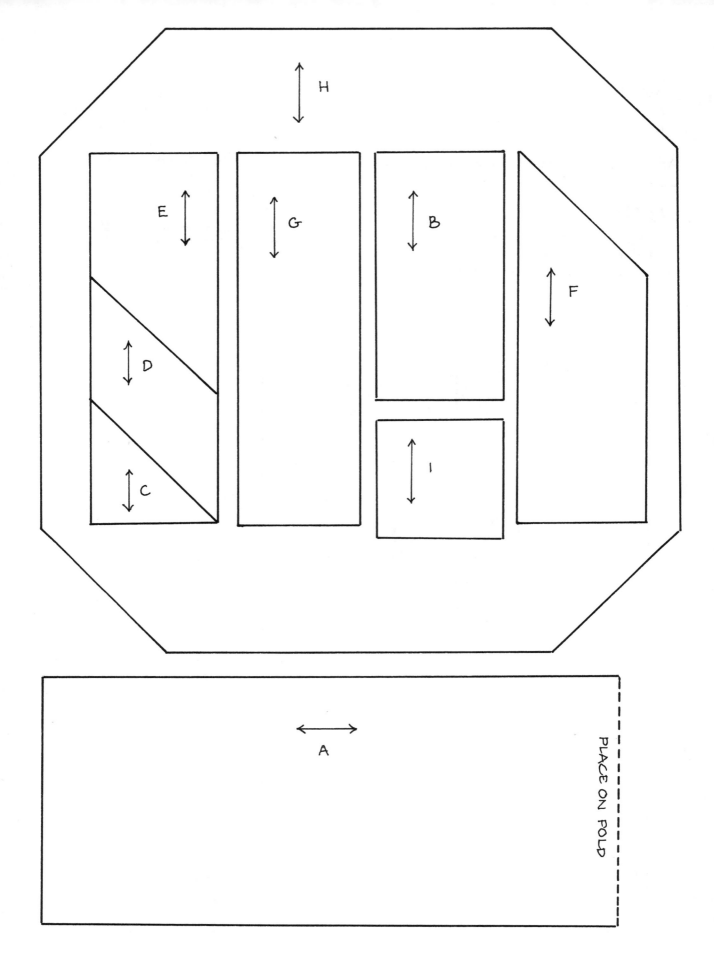

PLACE ON FOLD

42

6.
Coffeepot and Cup

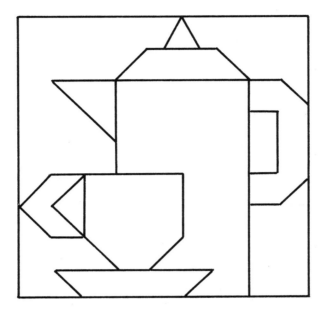

The 12" Coffeepot and Cup block is very easy to do and requires fourteen pattern pieces, A-N. This is a good beginner's pattern. All pattern pieces are actual size. About ⅓ yard (30.5 cm) of solid and print fabric is suggested.

The Coffeepot and Cup block looks best if the value of the cup and saucer is darker or brighter in color than the pot, giving the illusion of being in front of the pot. Quilted steam "vapor" rising from the pot lip adds a nice touch. The design is shown in color on page 67 and is included in the Town and Country Sampler quilt illustrated on page 115.

Assembling the Block

1. Cut all of the necessary pattern pieces, adding a ¼" seam allowance.

2. Using the illustrations and diagrams as a guide, piece the sections together in rows.

Row 1: Top section. A + C; J + J to I; F; G + C.
Row 2: Middle section. B, E, D; H+C; F+F.

Row 3: Bottom section, moving left to right. C + C to K; C + C to K; add on F; C + C to L; N; add on H, M, H. Then add H + C to N.

Your block is now complete.

Option

Shiny fabric may be used to suggest a glass knob on the pot cover (pattern piece I).

43

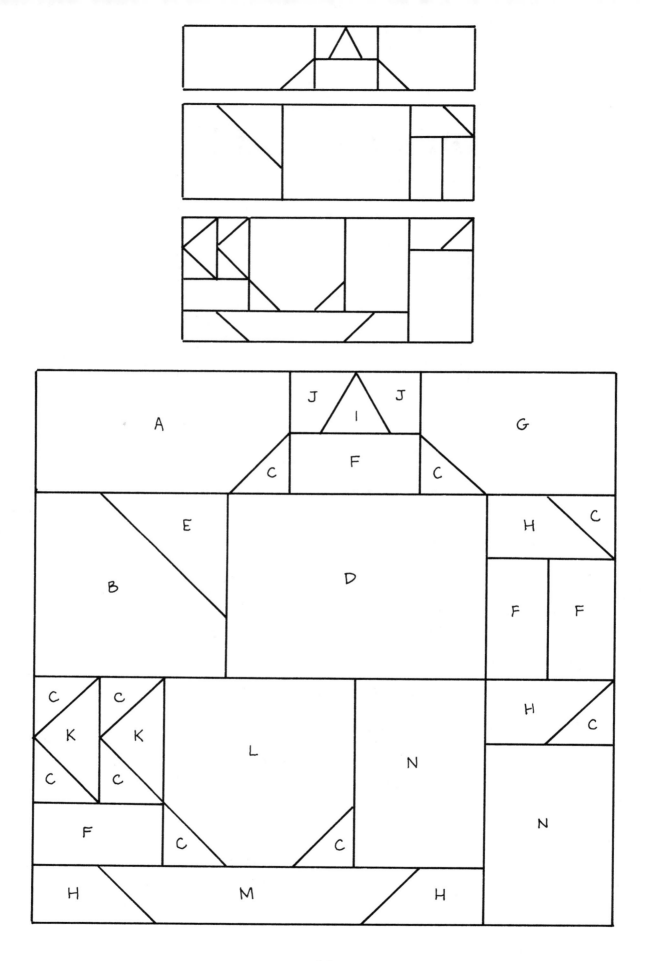

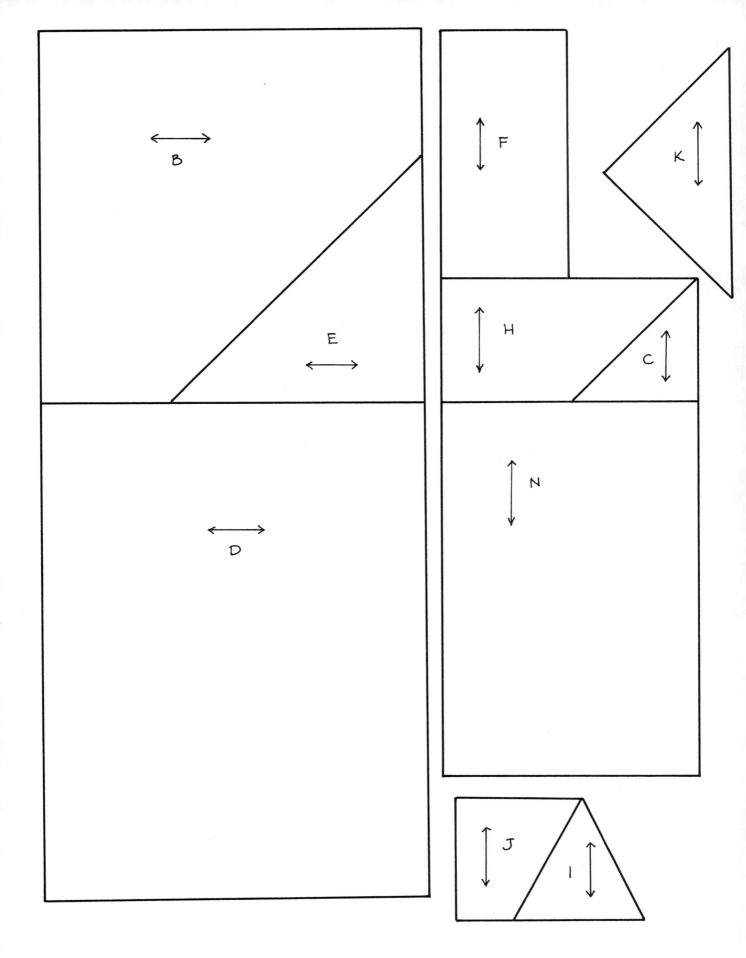

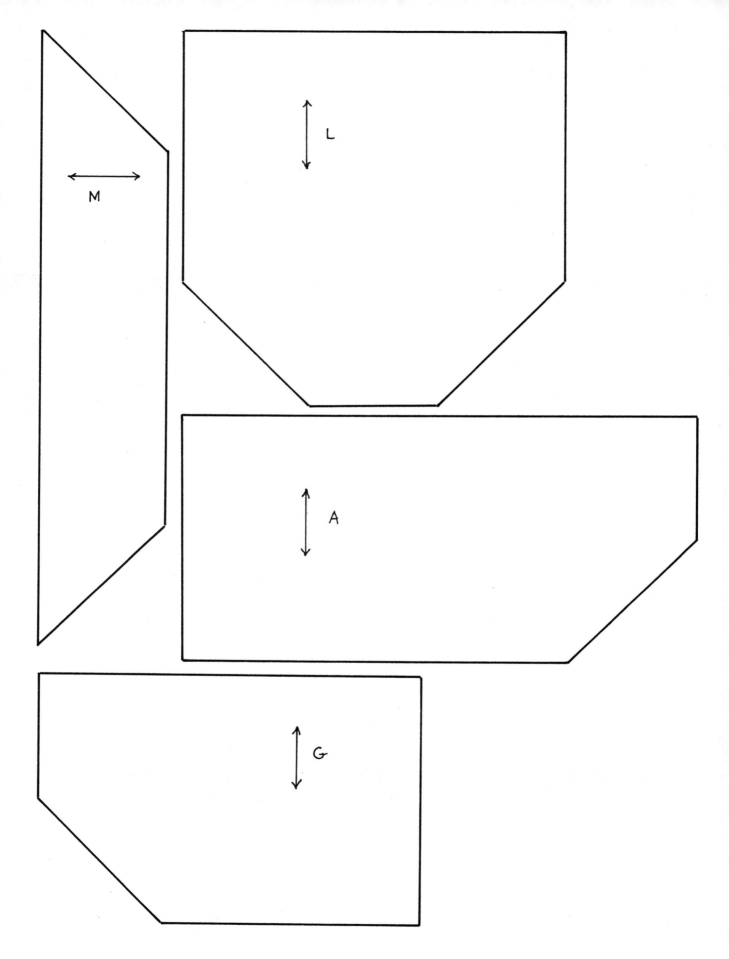

7.

Bowl and Pitcher

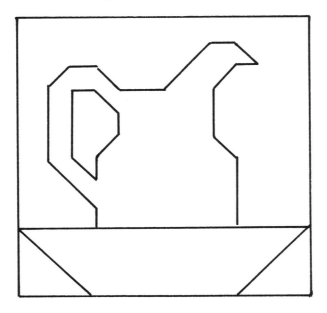

The 12" Bowl and Pitcher block is an easy-to-do pattern suitable for beginners. There are eighteen pattern pieces, A-R. All pattern pieces are actual size. About ⅓ yard (30.5 cm) of print and solid fabric is required. Calico print fabric is recommended for this design, although other prints and solids can be used. The Bowl and Pitcher block is shown in color on page 68 and is included in the Country Morning quilt project illustrated on page 116 and in the Town and Country Sampler quilt shown on page 115.

Assembling the Block

1. Cut all of the necessary pattern pieces, adding a ¼" seam allowance.

2. Using the illustrations and diagrams as a guide, sew the sections together in rows.

Row 1: At the bottom. R, Q, R.
Row 2: Top section, left side. A; C + D; E + E; B then C + L to M.
Row 3: Middle of top section, left side. G + F + D; then H + J; add N; then I + D + G; then at the bottom, C + C to O.
Row 4: Top section, right side. C + K; add on P.

The block is now complete.

Option

The 6" diagram has a few small pieces but can double as a pattern for a mini-wall quilt or for small projects such as potholders.

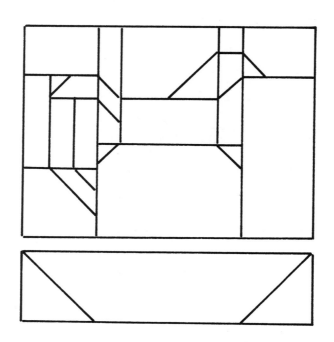

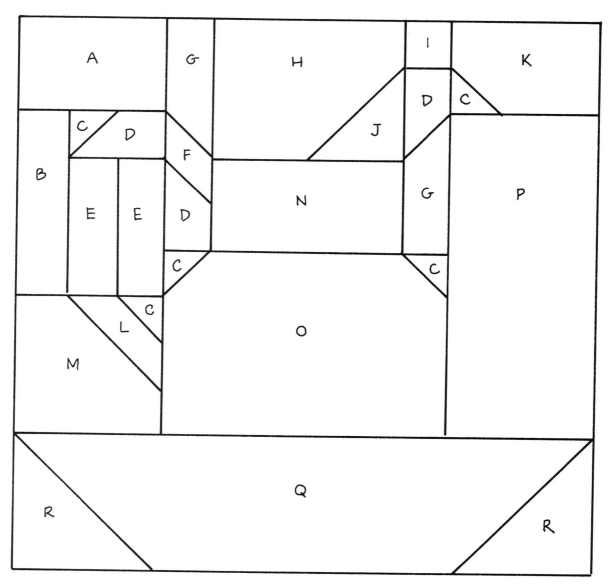

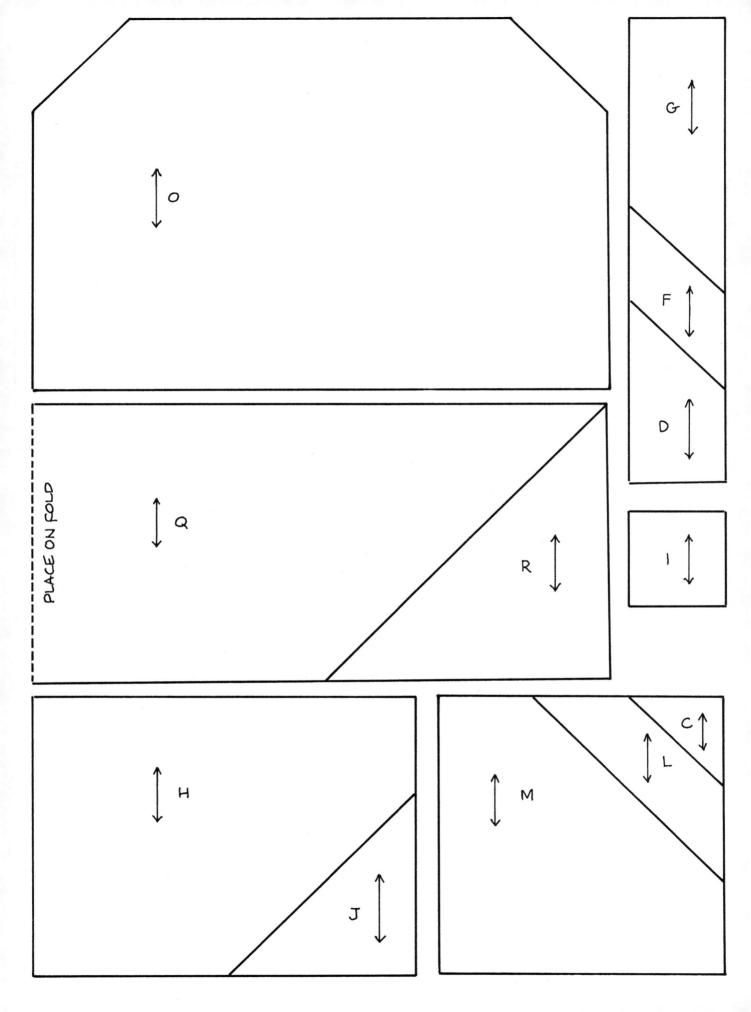

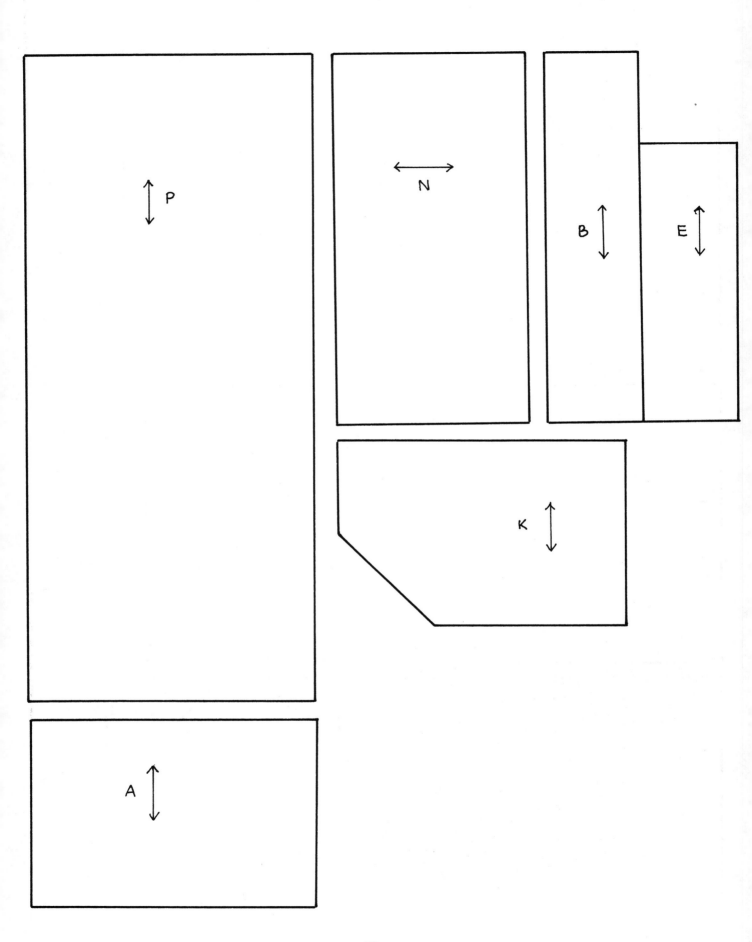

8.

Blue Jay

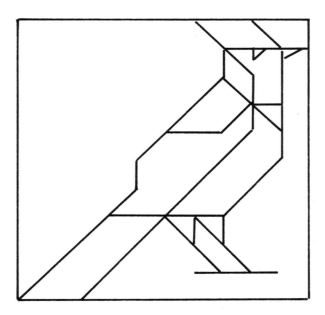

The 12" Blue Jay block is easy to do and requires eighteen pattern pieces, A-R. All pattern pieces are actual size. About ⅓ yard (30.5 cm) of solid and print cotton is needed. Feather patterns can be added using fabric paint (see Christmas Tree block). The colors shown in the illustration of the Blue Jay block on page 68 represent the true colors of the bird. Zigzag the legs and feet by machine (see the section on machine embroidery in Introduction and Instructions). This lovely block is included in the Town and Country Sampler project illustrated in color on page 115.

Assembling the Block

1. Cut all the necessary pattern pieces, adding a ¼" seam allowance.

2. Using the illustrations and diagrams as a guide, piece the sections together in rows.

Row 1: Starting at the bottom section.
   O, P, O; C + C + C + C to Q; add N.
Row 2: Top section. A + C; then bottom of midsection. C + D + C, then C + C, then L + M. Add K and K and R.

Row 3: Right of top section, left side. B, then C, E, D.
Row 4: D + C; C + F + C; I + G; H + J.

Your block is now complete.

Option

You can purchase rickrack and top stitch it in place to represent the bottom part of the legs and feet.

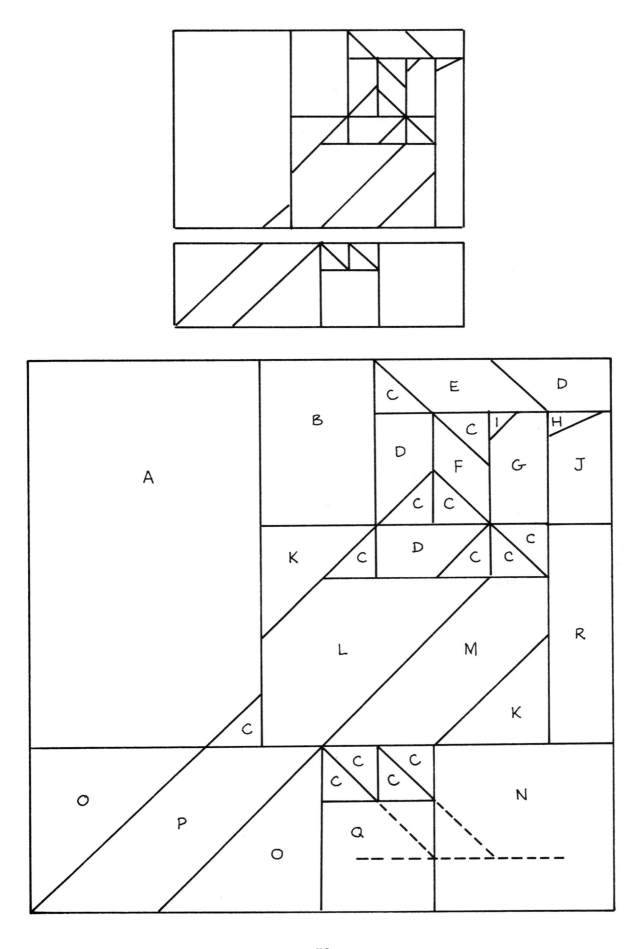

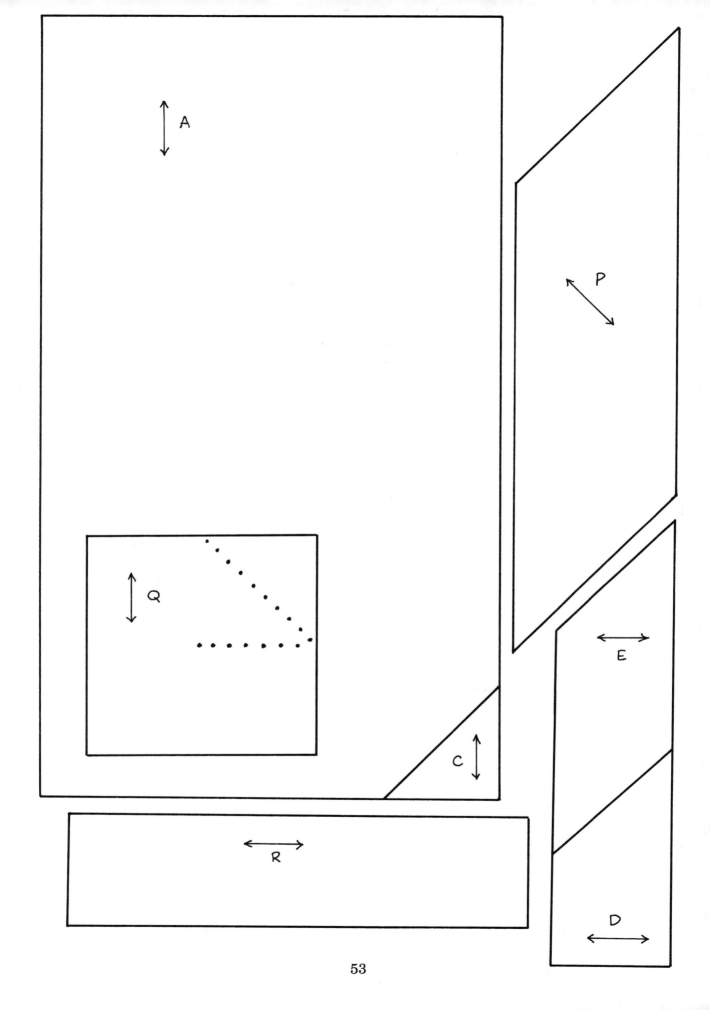

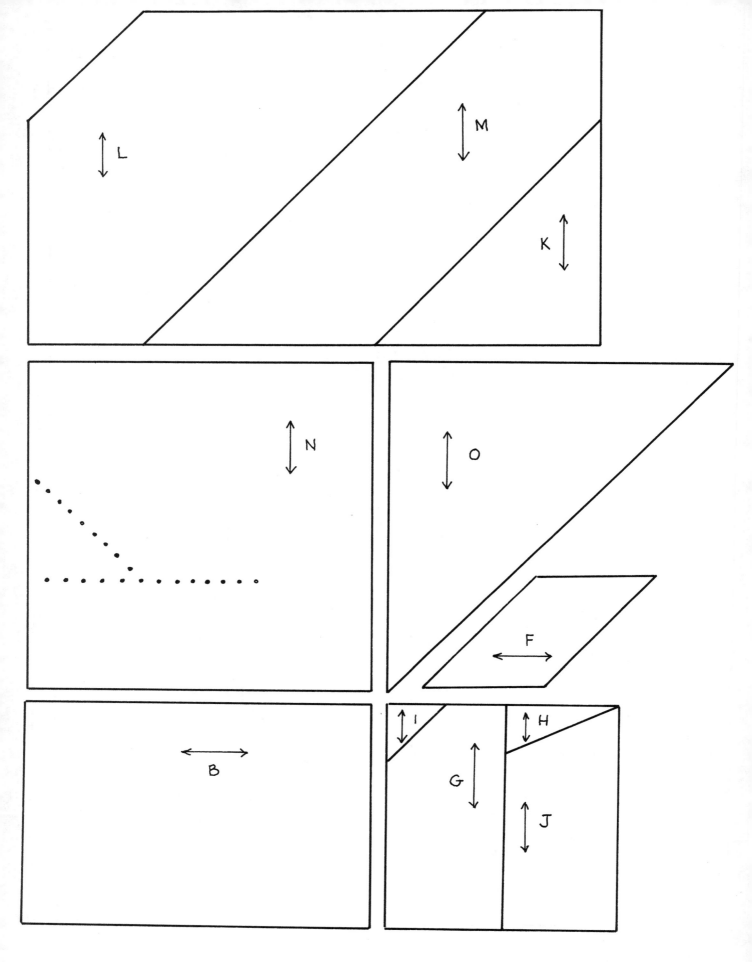

9.
Oil Lamp

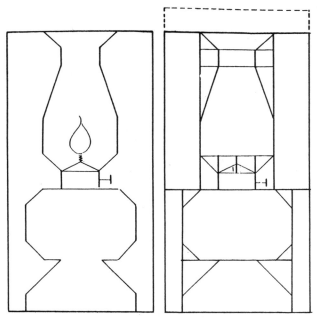

The double-size 12" by 24" Oil Lamp block is moderately easy to do and uses fourteen pattern pieces, A-N. All pattern pieces are actual size. About $\frac{1}{3}$ yard (30.5 cm) of solid and large pattern fabric is suggested. The flame is added by using fabric paint (see Christmas Tree block). The Oil Lamp block gives a nice change of size in a quilt that has all 12" blocks. Feel free to use fabrics of unusual design balance in this block. A large asymmetric flower in the middle section of the lamp, as shown in the illustration on page 115, makes a very attractive design. The small knob that turns the wick can be zigzag or top stitched by machine.

If you are placing this block in a quilt with sashes, it is necessary to add the width of the sash to the top of the block to make it fit with the other 12" blocks. Without sashes, this adjustment is not needed. The dash lines on the diagram indicate where the sash adjustment is added. A cool-color background looks good with this design. The Oil Lamp block design is shown in color on page 69 and is included in the Town and Country Sampler shown on page 115.

Assembling the Block

1. Cut all the necessary pattern pieces, adding a $\frac{1}{4}$" seam allowance.

2. Using the illustrations and diagrams as a guide, piece the sections together in rows.

Row 1: Top section, between the two A's. C + B + C.
Row 2: D + E + D.
Row 3: F + G + F.
Row 4: C + J; H + I to H + I; add on E; C + J. Add an A to each side.

Row 5: Bottom section, between the two L's. C + C + C + C to K.

Row 6: N + N to M. Add an L to each side.

Your block is now complete.

Options

As an alternative, you can appliqué or stencil the flame. If the Oil Lamp block is to be very decorative, say for a Christmas quilt, you might like to try a small amount of gold fabric for the flame, which is appliquéd using fusible transfer web (see Angel block). Added to that, you can top stitch circular lines in gold metallic or nylon thread around it. Do this before the quilt sandwich is made. If your machine breaks the metallic thread, you will have to do this by hand.

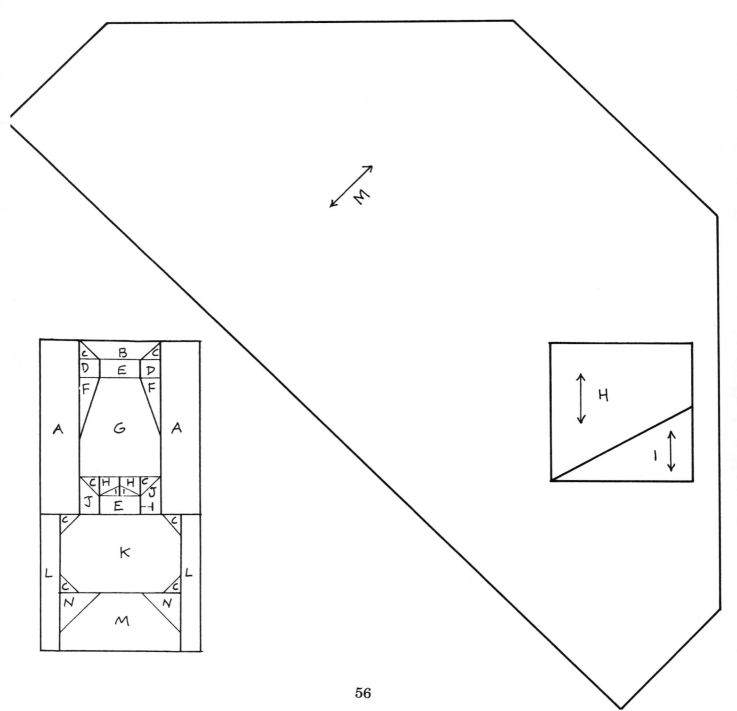

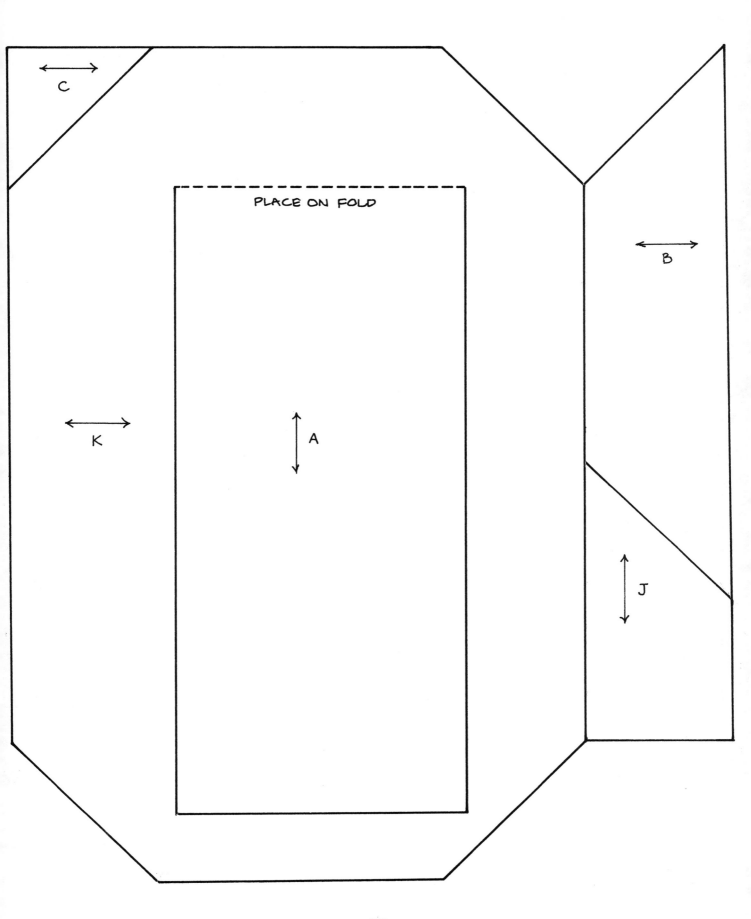

PLACE ON FOLD

C

B

K

A

J

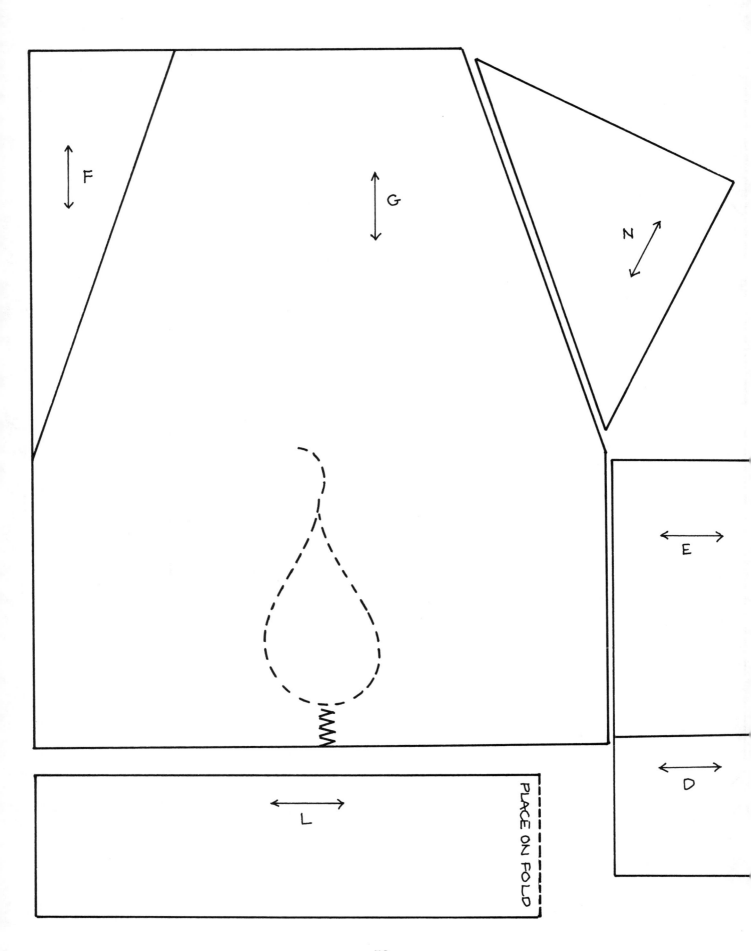

F

G

N

E

D

L

PLACE ON FOLD

10.
Coffee Grinder

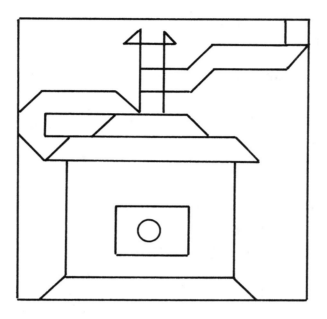

The 12" Coffee Grinder block is moderately easy to do and requires nineteen pattern pieces, A-S. All pattern pieces are actual size. About ⅓ yard (30.5 cm) of fabric is needed. Brown and coffee-color print and solid fabric add to that "coffee feeling." As evocative early American images, the Coffee Grinder, Pineapple, and Bowl and Pitcher designs will complement each other in a country-style quilt.

Pattern piece J has dash lines indicating where that shape is top stitched or quilted. This is the area where the crank is found on a real coffee grinder. The crank could be done also with separate piecing, but it is easier to top stitch or quilt, and it gives almost the same results. Top stitching saves you having to piece twice more for the same effect. The drawer knob is easy to appliqué, using fusible transfer web. The Coffee Grinder block is shown in color on page 69 and is included in the Town and Country Sampler illustrated on page 115.

Assembling the Block

1. Cut all the necessary pattern pieces, adding a ¼" seam allowance.

2. Using the illustrations and diagrams as a guide, piece the sections together in rows.

Row 1: Bottom section, starting in the middle. Q, Q + S, J. Add on N, N, and P. Then on the left side, add on M + C, and on the right side, O + C.

Row 2: Middle section. C, R, L, D.

Row 3: Top section, starting at the bottom left side. E, D, K, C.

Row 4: C + B to A.

Row 5: Middle of top section. H + I, D + C.

Row 6: E, J.
Row 7: H + I, E, E, E.
Row 8: F, G, F.
Row 9: Right side of top section. J, E.
Row 10: B, C, then add A.
Your block is now complete.

Option

An easy alternative to appliqué for the drawer knob is to sew on an attractive button.

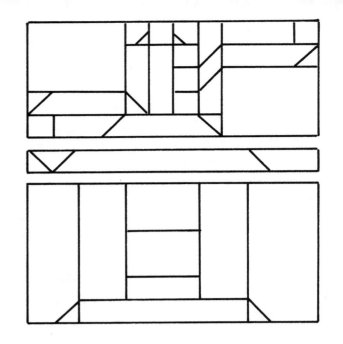

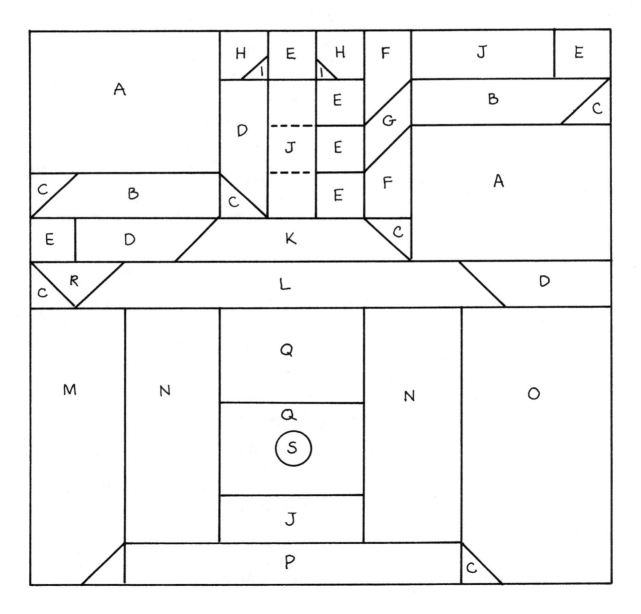

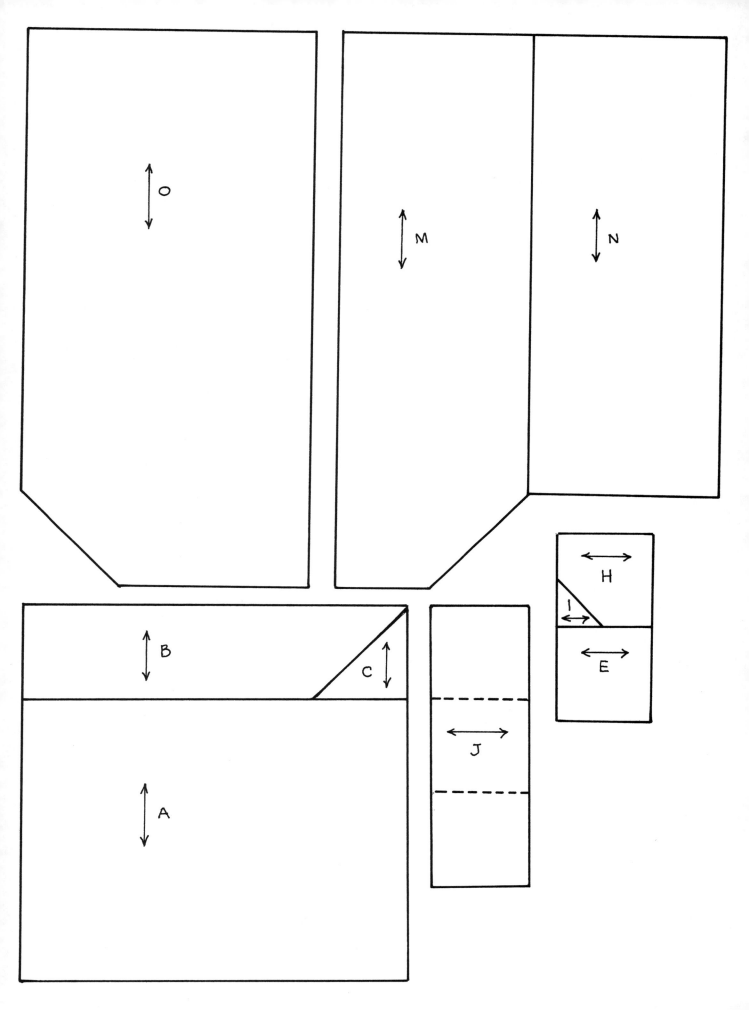

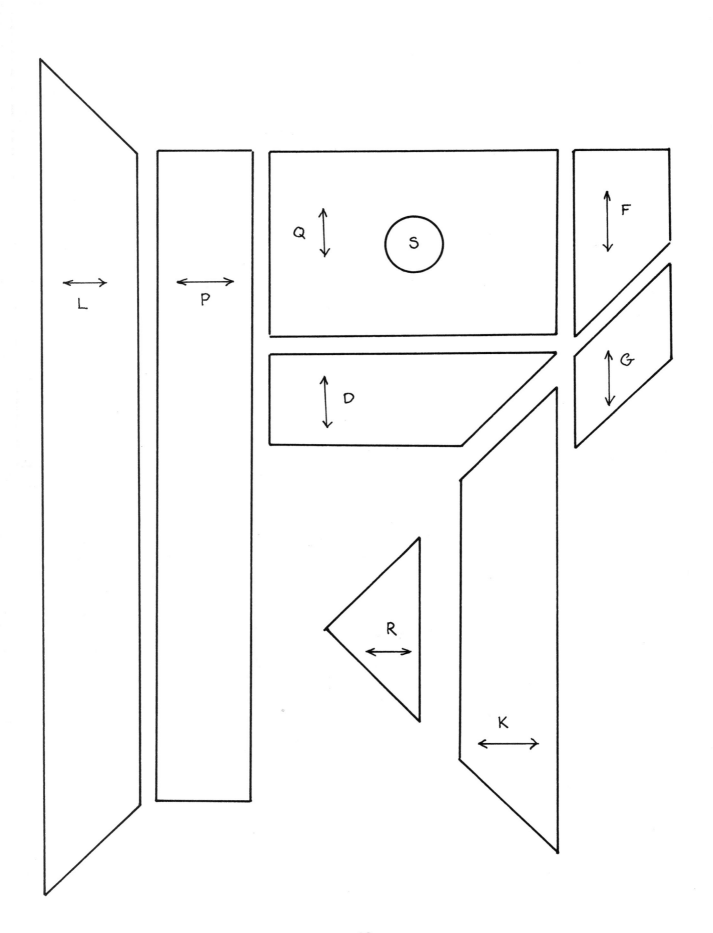

11.
Baby Duck

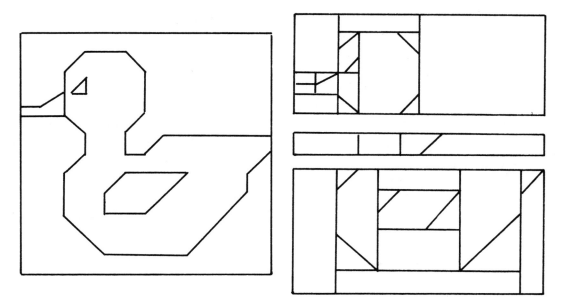

The 12" Baby Duck block is moderately easy to do and requires twenty-two pattern pieces, A-V. All pattern pieces are actual size. About ⅓ yard (30.5 cm) of solid and print fabric is needed. The baby duck in pastel color prints makes a charming block. This design is shown in color on page 70 and is included in the Town and Country Sampler illustrated on page 115.

Assembling the Block

1. Cut all of the necessary pattern pieces, adding a ¼" seam allowance.

2. Using the illustrations and diagrams as a guide, piece the sections together in rows.

  Row 1: Bottom section, starting to the right of O. C, P, R.
  Row 2: B, C + Q + R, V, S + T.
  Row 3: Add U to the bottom. Add O and C + N to the sides.
  Row 4: Middle section. L, J, E, N.
  Row 5: Top section, starting left to right. A, H + H, F + G, J.
  Row 6: C + D + I; E + C.

  Row 7: C + C to K. Add on B and M.

Your block is now complete.

Options

You can do the duck with or without "water." On the diagram and patterns you will notice an optional dash line that goes across the design; this is the water line. You can give the illusion of water transparency if you want the bottom of the duck to appear to be in the water by using a fabric reactive dye on some of the fabric. There are several brand names on the market. Follow the manufacturer's directions carefully. You can do this with a dye bath, or you can paint it right on the fabric. Be sure to wear a mask when mixing the powder so you won't breathe it in. Also it is a good idea to wear gloves to protect your skin. Do a sample test with the fabric you plan to use before you do the block. To give the illusion of water, dye all the fabric shapes that will appear *below the water line.* Dye them a blue-green, the color of water. This can be done even with print fabrics and gives a fascinating effect.

Another method for giving the illusion of water is to use only the correct *middle* color of fabric. If your duck is yellow and the water is green,

the middle color is a mixture of the two (yellow-green). If your sky or background is blue and the water is green, the middle will be blue-green. It must be the correct color and value. With all the new rainbow fabrics on the market today, you might be able to find it.

The Baby Duck block can also serve as an *adult* duck by using more realistic fabric colors. If you don't use sashes, the ducks can be joined to "swim" in the same direction in one row and in the opposite in the next row (just reverse the template).

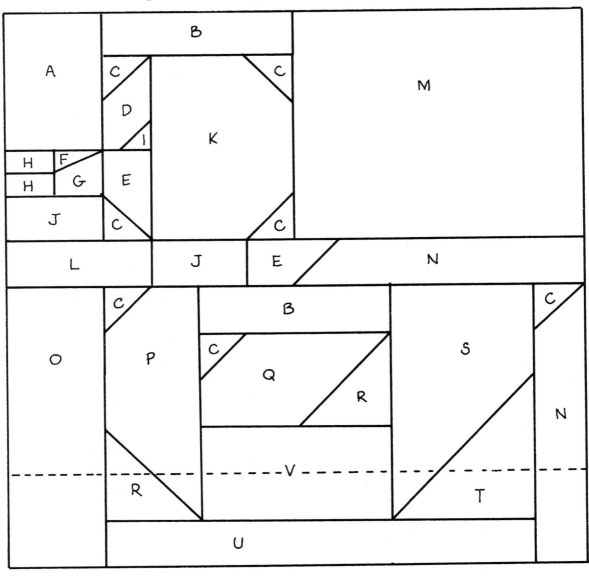

 Pattern pieces continued on page 73.

1. Christmas Tree

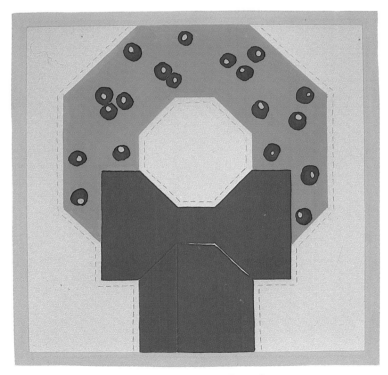

2. Christmas Wreath

3. Angel

4. Jam Jar

5. Pineapple

6. Coffeepot and Cup

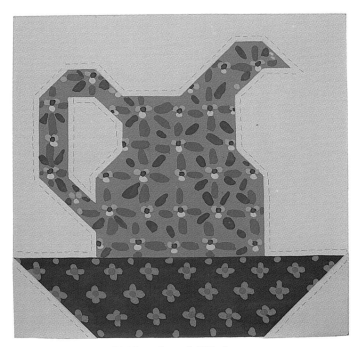

7. Bowl and Pitcher

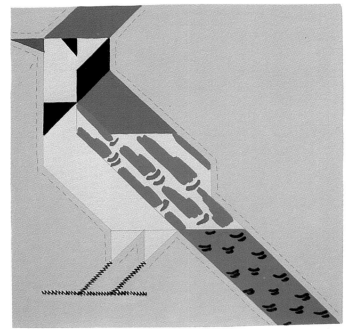

8. Blue Jay

9. Oil Lamp

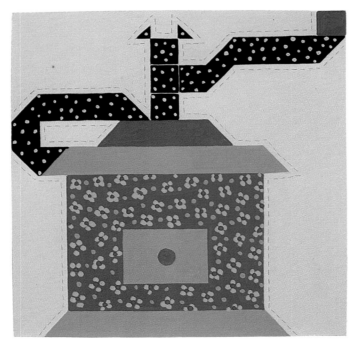

10. Coffee Grinder

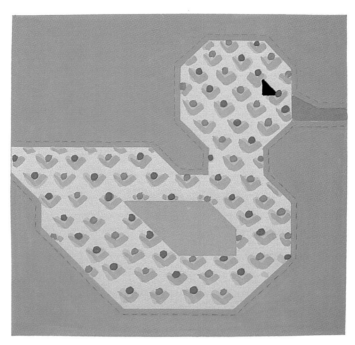

11. Baby Duck

12. Hen

70

13. Bird and Bath

14. Teapot

15. Crab

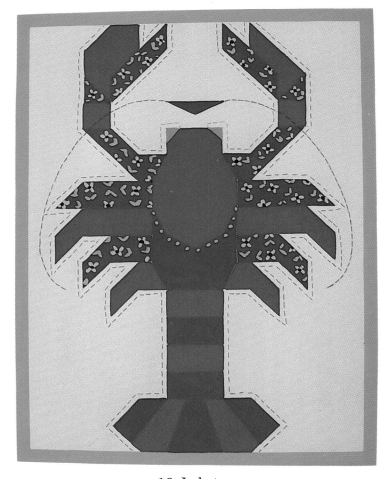

16. Lobster

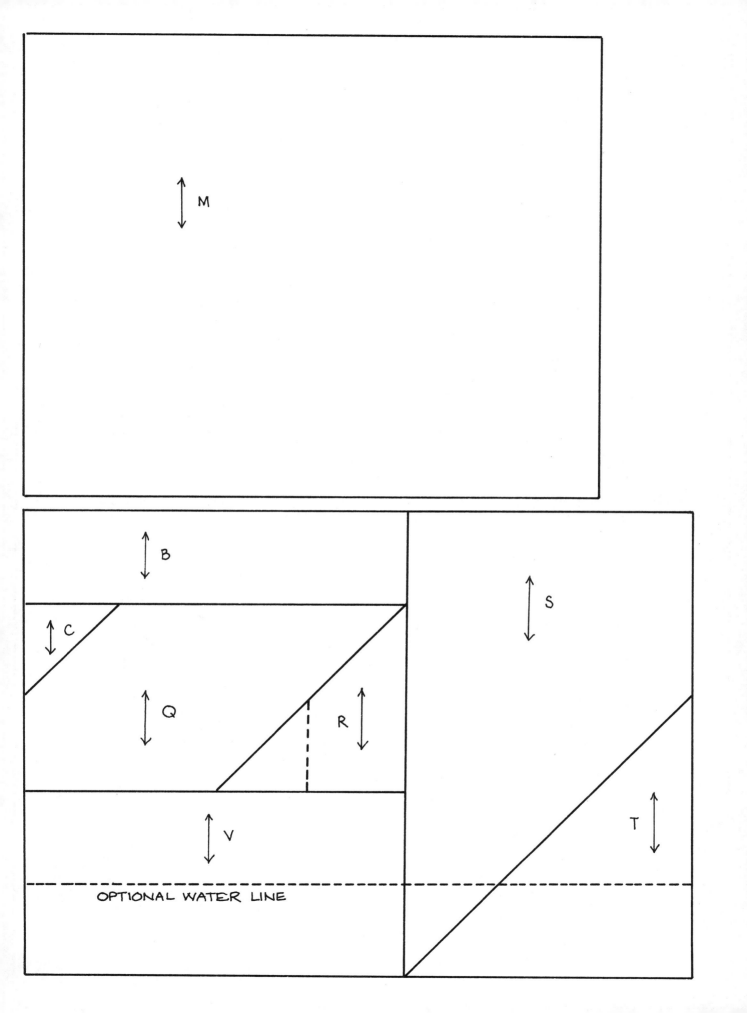

OPTIONAL WATER LINE

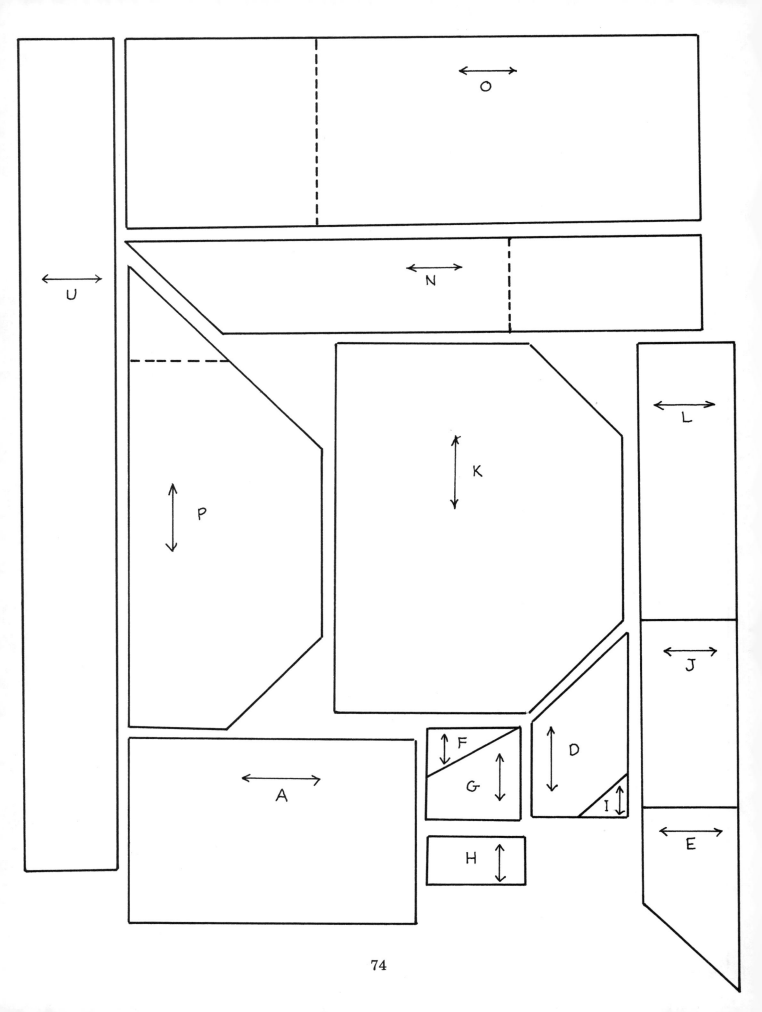

12.
Hen

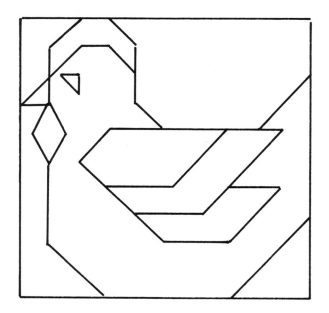

The 12" Hen Block is moderately easy to do and requires twenty-two pattern pieces, A-V. All pattern pieces are actual size. About ⅓ yard (30.5 cm) of solid and print cotton fabric is suggested. A little more piecing is required for this block, but the results are worth it. The hen might be a little red, white, brown, or even a colorful scrap-fabric bird. Careful choice of fabric will give it a contemporary or a country look. This design block is shown in color on page 70 and is included in the Town and Country Sampler illustrated on page 115.

Assembling the Block

1. Cut all of the necessary pattern pieces, adding a ¼" seam allowance.

2. Using the illustrations and diagrams as a guide, sew the sections together in rows.

> *Row 1*: Bottom section. U, M; N + O and N, P; add on Q, then add on S and S.
> *Row 2*: Middle section, moving left to right. E + F + F; D + D; C + C to R, K, L.
> *Row 3*: Top section, left side. E + F + F;

> A + C; C, B, C; T + I.
> *Row 4*: Top section, starting in the middle, moving left to right. D + D; B + C + C; J; G + C; H + V.

Your block is now complete.

Options

The comb on top of the hen's head can have added texture by top stitching red rickrack on the top edge. Feather effects on her body can be suggested with top stitching or quilting.

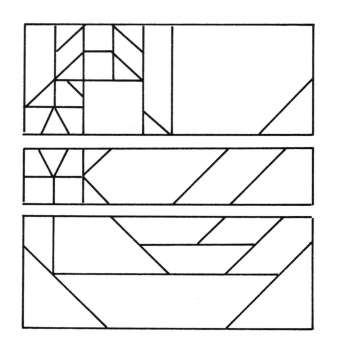

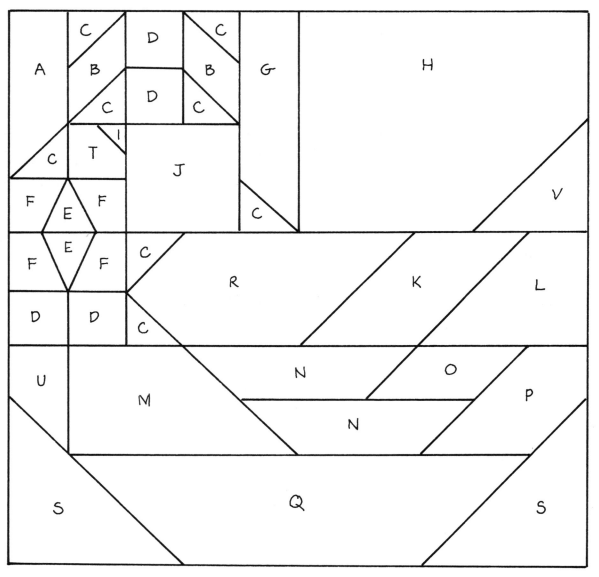

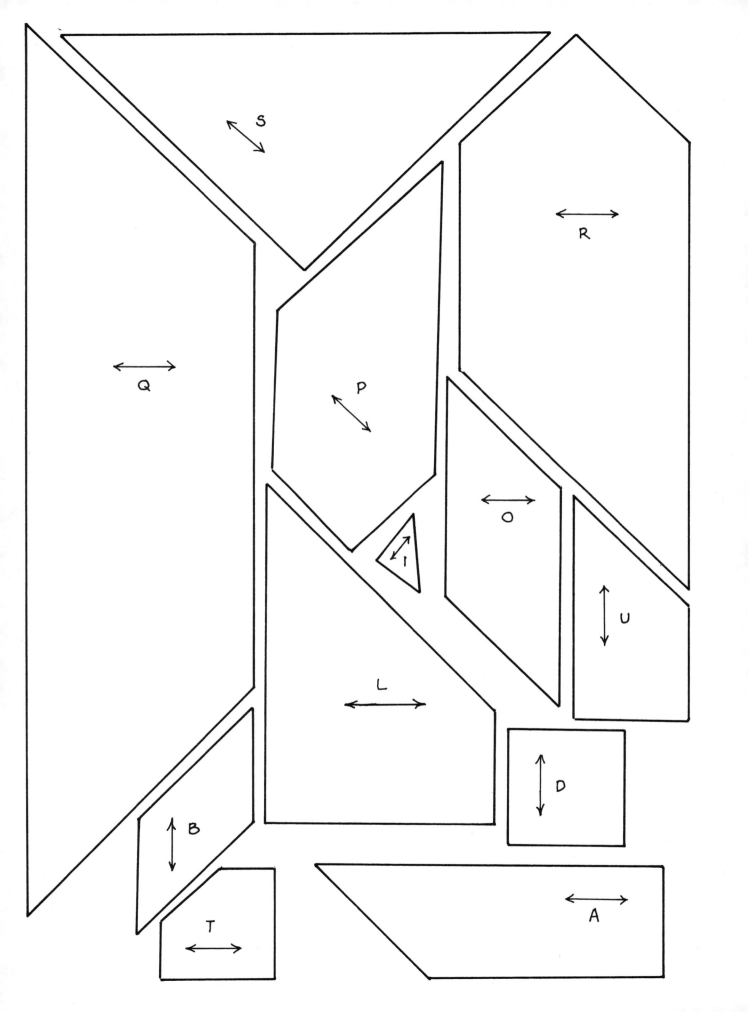

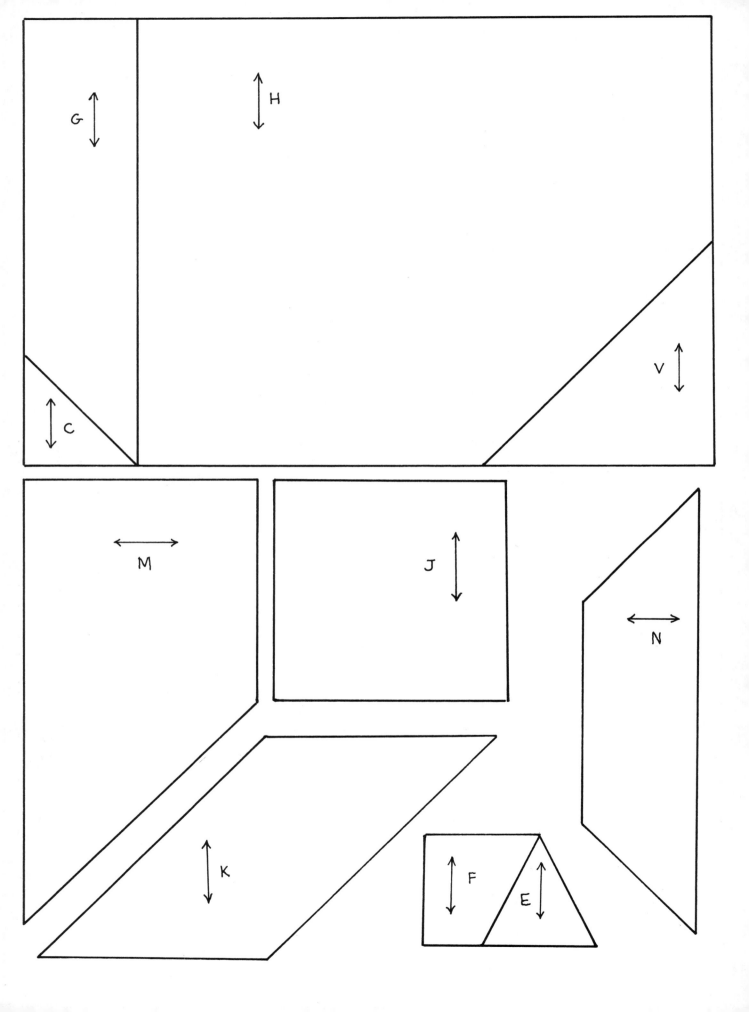

13.
Bird and Bath

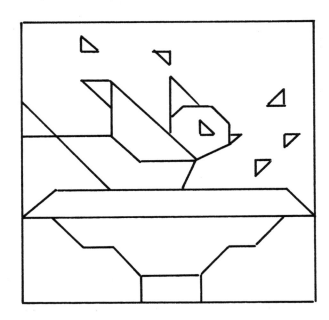

The Bird and Bath block is moderately easy to do and requires twenty-two pattern pieces, A-V. All pattern pieces are actual size. About ⅓ yard (30.5 cm) of print and solid-color cotton is needed. This design makes a very attractive and colorful block. It is shown in color on page 71 and is included in the Town and Country Sampler illustrated on page 115.

Assembling the Block

1. Cut all of the necessary pattern pieces, adding a ¼" seam allowance.

2. Using the illustrations and diagrams as a guide, sew the sections together in rows.

Row 1: Bottom section, moving left to right. H + C; F; V + C; T, F; F; C + V; C + H.
Row 2: Moving up. C, S, C.
Row 3: Middle, moving left to right. M; N + N; O + P; Q to R; I + G; B; I + J; I + G.

Row 4: Top section, moving left to right. A + C; I + J; B; C + D; then F; G + I; E + E.
Row 5: H + C; I + J; I + I to U.
Row 6: K + I; add on L and L.

Your block is now complete.

Option

The five water drops (triangles) around the bird look great if you use a shiny ice-blue or blue-green fabric to give the illusion of water.

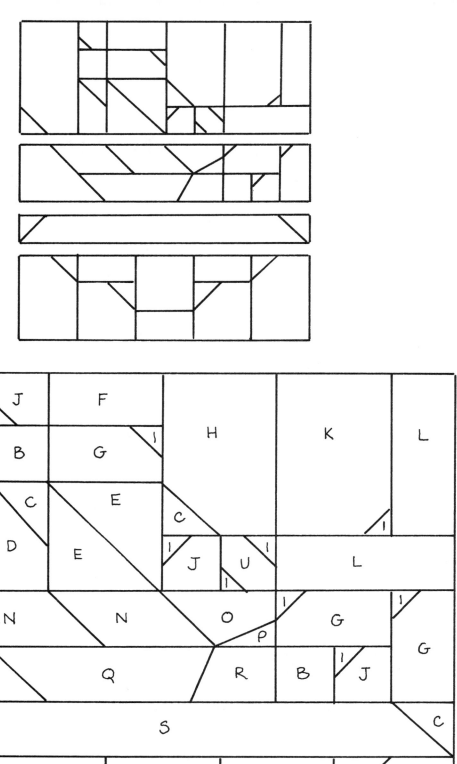

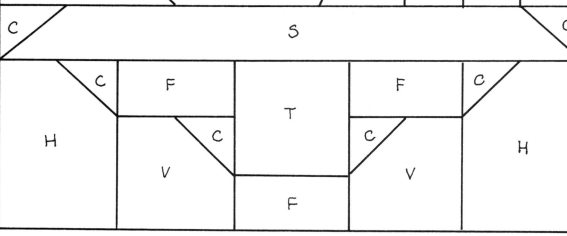

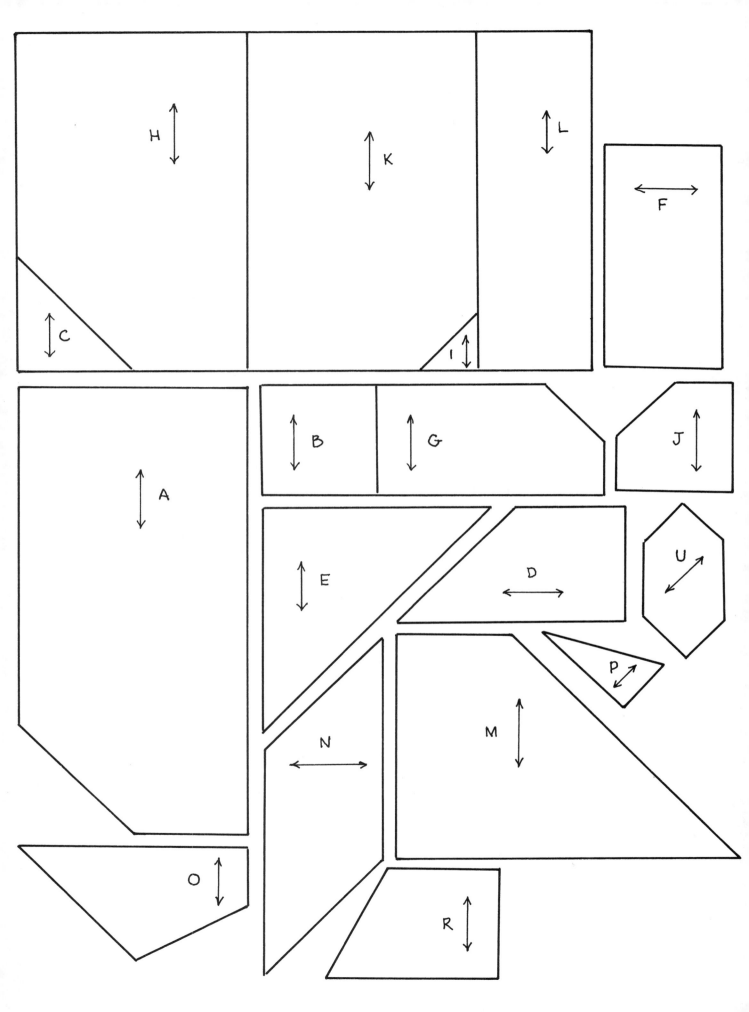

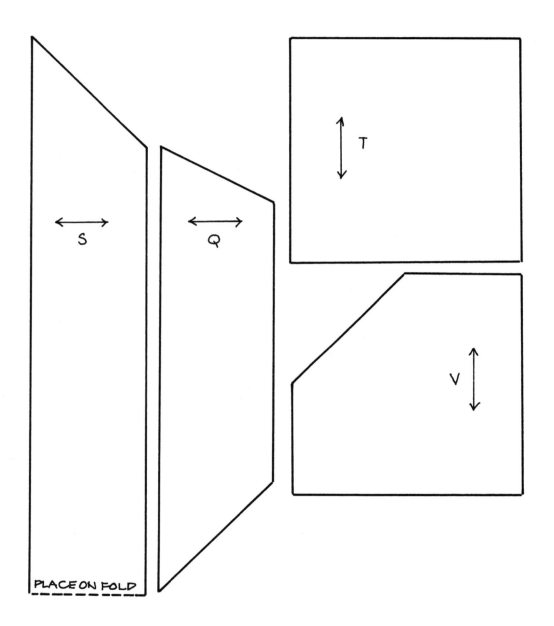

S

Q

T

V

PLACE ON FOLD

14.
Teapot

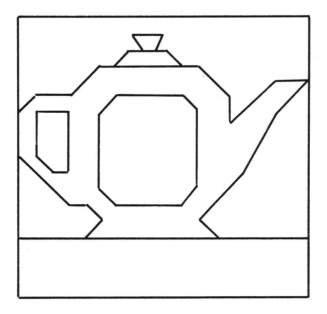

The 12" Teapot block is for the quilter who has had some previous experience as it has twenty-six pattern pieces, A-Z. All pattern pieces are actual size. About ⅓ yard (30.5) of solid and print fabric is needed.

The center panel is a fine place to use that "special" fabric with unusual pattern, texture, or color. Large flower prints, cut so that the flower is placed attractively, can make a pretty teapot. The lid can match, as shown in the color illustration on page 71. This design is also included in the Town and Country Sampler on page 115.

Assembling the Block

1. Cut all of the necessary pattern pieces, adding a ¼" seam allowance.

2. Using the illustrations and diagrams as a guide, sew the sections together in rows.

Row 1: Left section, moving from top to bottom. A; C + L; T + B; U + V + E; O.

Row 2: Middle section, starting at the top. D + C; G; I + I to H; G; D + C.

Row 3: Middle section, left side. E, S; C + C to P.

Row 4: Middle. N; C + C + C + C to Q; N.

Row 5: Middle section, right side. E, M; R + C.

Row 6: Right side. X, Y, J; C + L; then E, K; add on F and A. Add Z to the bottom.

Your block is now complete.

Options

The center panel can be used or not, as you wish. If you decide not to use it, the optional tea bag tag (W) can be used as an added touch of color. The string attaching the tag (dotted line) can be hand embroidered, top-stitched by machine, or just attached 3-D style at the top and bottom with decorative cord. Fabric shops have a good selection to choose from.

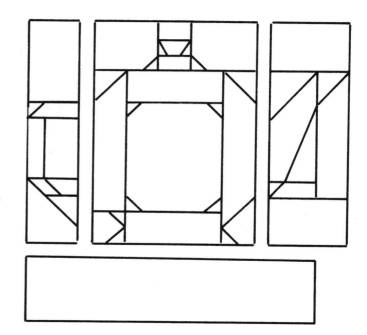

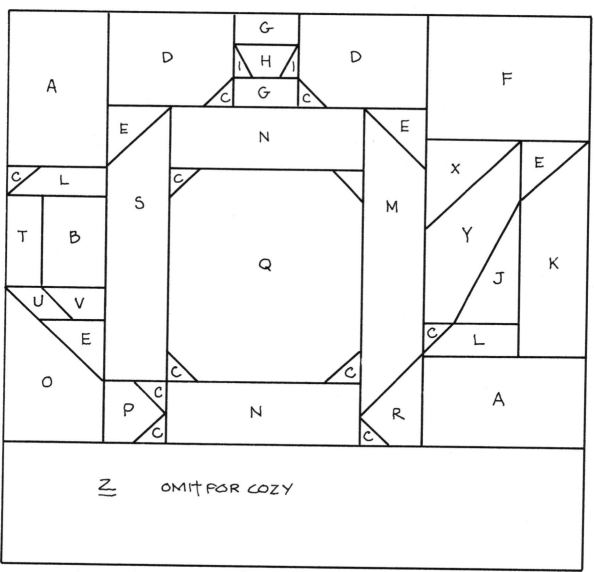

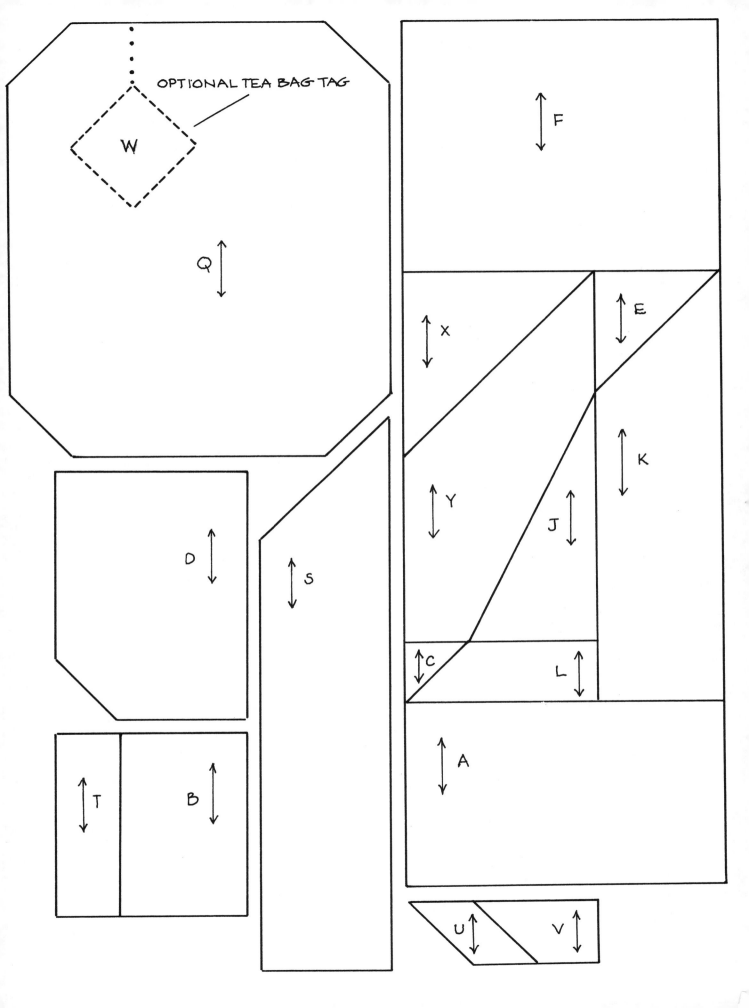

OPTIONAL TEA BAG TAG

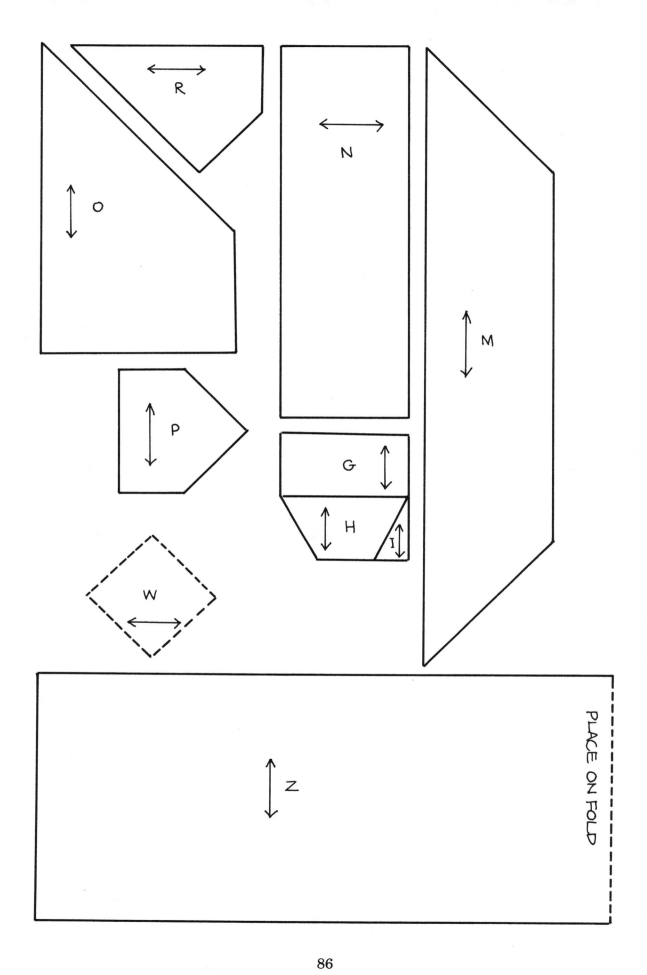

15.
Crab

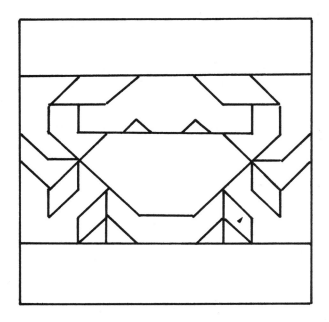

The 12" Crab block is moderately easy to do and requires fourteen pattern pieces, A-N. About ⅓ yard (30.5 cm) of solid and print fabric is required. All pattern pieces are actual size. This is a lovely design for using nice prints from the scrap fabric that most quilters have accumulated. Any combination of colors can be used. I have suggested a deep rose print and solid fabric for the crab pictured in color on page 72, with a cream-color background. The A pattern (top and bottom) gives an additional area for color.

Assembling the Block

1. Cut all of the necessary pattern pieces, adding a ¼" seam allowance.

2. Using the illustrations and diagrams as a guide, sew the sections together in rows.

Row 1: Starting near the top. B, C, D, C, B.
Row 2: Moving down. E, E; F + I; I and I to H; F + I; E, E.
Row 3: Leg section, left side. J + M; J + K + B; L + K + J; J + K; L + L.
Row 4: Body. J + J to G; J + J; N; J + J .

Row 5 : Leg section, right side. J + K + L ; B + K + J ; J + M. Add on K + J. Add on L + L. Add A to the top and bottom to complete the block.

Options

Pattern A can be doubled and used *either* on the top or on the bottom of the crab instead of on both. Fabric that resembles water and/or sand and shells can replace the split A for a colorful, decorative effect.

If you eliminate pattern A altogether, the

smaller narrow block can be joined in rows for an ideal seaside border on a nautical quilt. This pattern is excellent for a scrap or "charm" (all prints different from one another, no two the same) quilt of any size.

The Crab block, however you decide to use it, can become a Cancer the Crab design for your favorite "Moonchild" born under that sign.

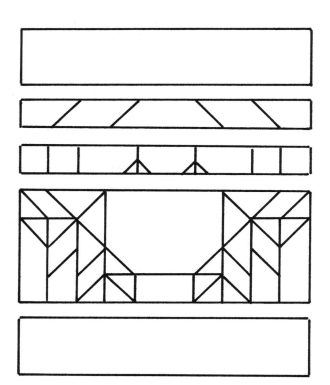

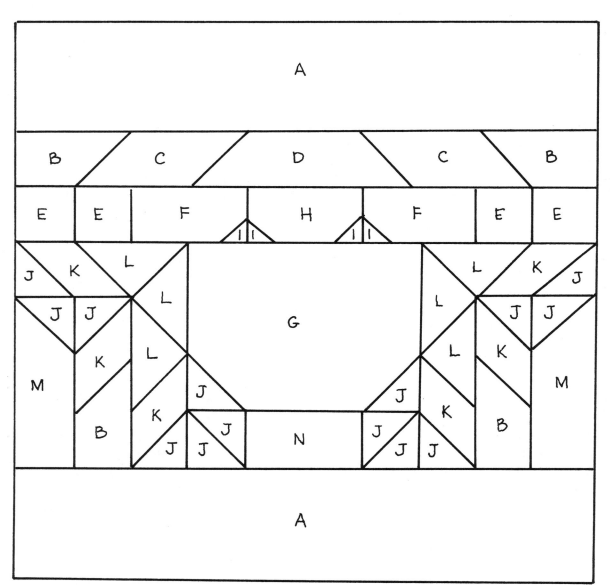

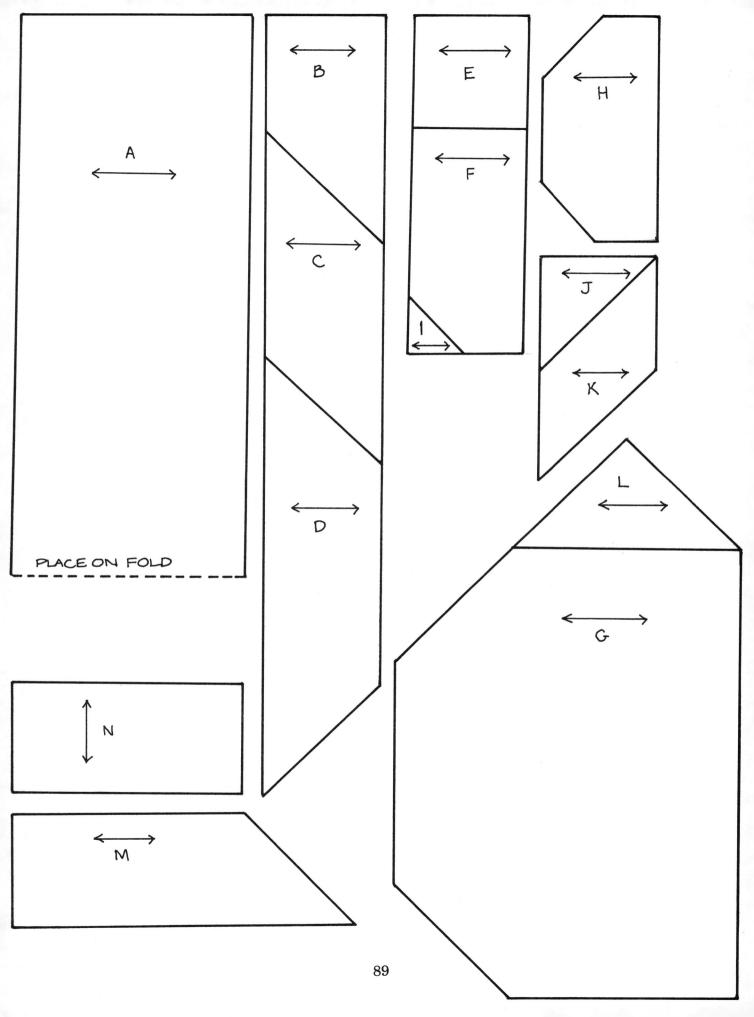

A

B

C

D

PLACE ON FOLD

E

F

I

H

J

K

L

G

N

M

16.
Lobster

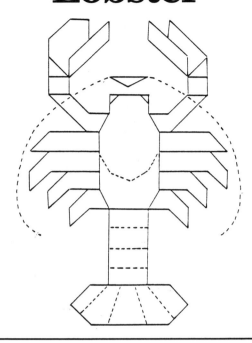

The double size 12" by 24" Lobster block is a challenge for the advanced quilter as it has twenty-five pattern pieces, A-Y, many of which are small. All pattern pieces are actual size. About ¼ yard (30.5 cm) or 12" by 24" (30.5 cm by 61 cm) of scrap fabric is needed. You will have fabric left over. Without sashes the 12" by 24" size will fit with all of the other 12" blocks. The block is shown in color on page 72, and a variation of the design is used in the Lobster Bib project illustrated on page 114.

Assembling the Block

1. Cut all of the necessary pattern pieces, adding a ¼" seam allowance.

2. The arrows on the diagram indicate where the sections are joined.

3. Using the illustrations and the diagrams as a guide, piece the sections together in rows.

Row 1: Starting at the bottom. V; C + C + C + C to W; V.
Row 2: Moving up. U, B, U.
Row 3: Moving up. T, C, D, S, D, C, T.
Row 4: Moving up. S, C, K, N, O, N, K, C, S.
Row 5: Moving up. M + C + K + R; then above, D + Q; then above, D + Q; add to P.
Row 6: Right side of P, starting at the bottom. R + K + C + M; then Q + D and Q + D.
Row 7: Moving up to next section . D, N, O, N, D .
Row 8: Moving up. C, K, D; I + I to J, D, K, C.
Row 9: Top left claw, moving down. C, E, C, M; then D, C, G, F.
Row 10: Above eyes. B; H + L; H + L.
Row 11: Right claw, left side. C + K; G,

F; then Y + C + M; add X. Add A to each side of rows 7-11.

The Lobster block is now complete.

4. The antennae and body shell pattern, indicated by dash lines on the patterns, may be top stitched on by machine in a running, zigzag, or decorative stitch.

Option

This lobster will make an excellent scrap block, using a different red print for each pattern.

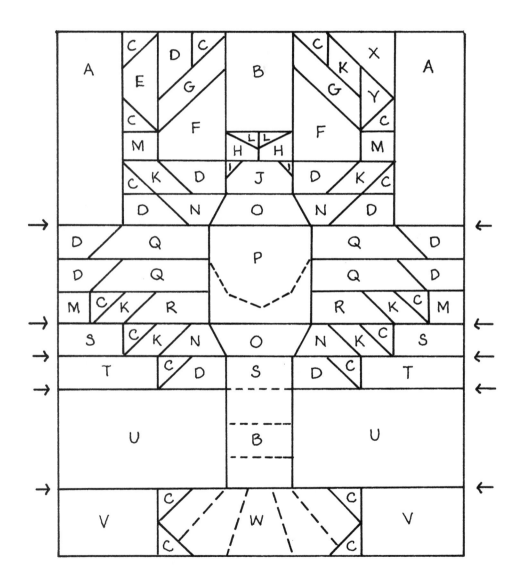

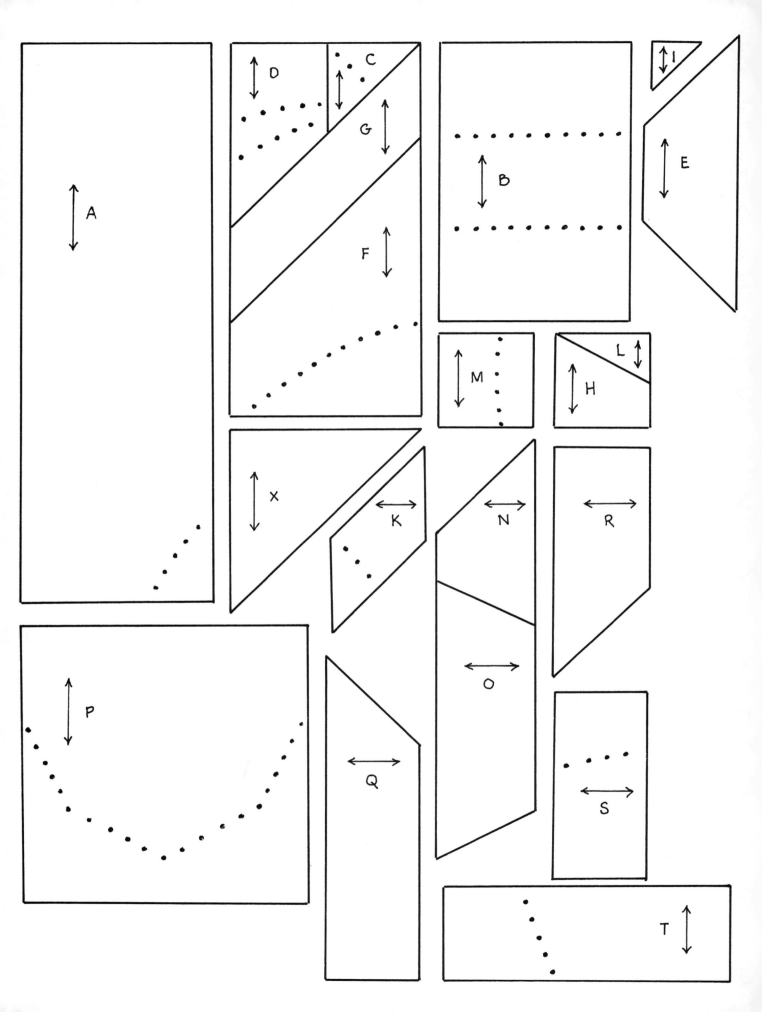

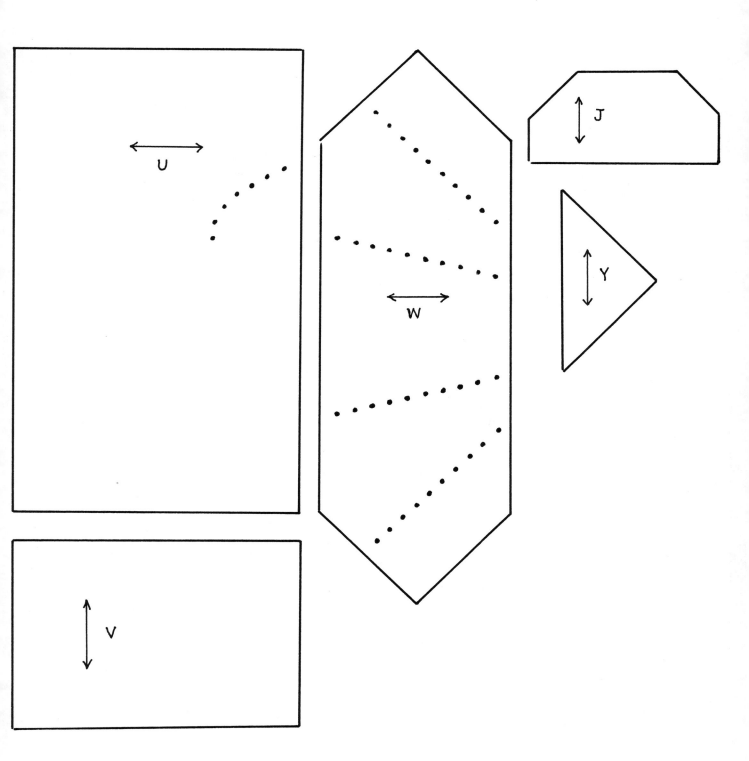

17.
Cat One

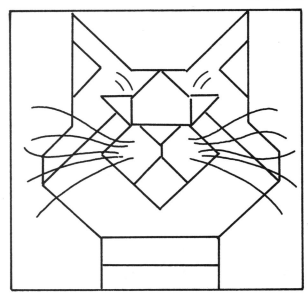 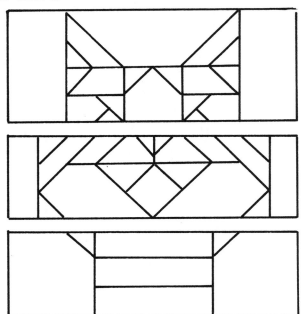

The 12" Cat One block is moderately easy to do and requires seventeen pattern pieces, A-Q. All pattern pieces are actual size. About ⅓ yard (30.5 cm) of solid and print cotton fabric is suggested. Whiskers look best in shiny white thread, top stitched on the block before it is quilted.

This black-and-white cat was designed after our cat, Harry. Your cat can be any color you wish. The block is included in The Cat's Meow quilt project shown in color on page 117.

Assembling the Block

1. Cut all of the necessary pattern pieces, adding a ¼" seam allowance.

2. Using the illustrations and diagrams as a guide, sew the sections together in rows.

Row 1: Starting at the top middle section, moving left to right. C + D; B; C + D.

Row 2: Bottom of top middle section. C + H, G + J to C; C + C to F; then H + C; G + J to C; add A to each side.

Row 3: Middle section, starting in the middle and moving towards the sides. I + K to E, and I + K to E.

Row 4: L + L to M; add on N + C and N + C. Add on D + C and D + C. Add O to each side.

Row 5: Bottom section. Q + C; P + P + P; Q + C.

The block is now complete. Whiskers may now be added (next to the mouth and over the eyes).

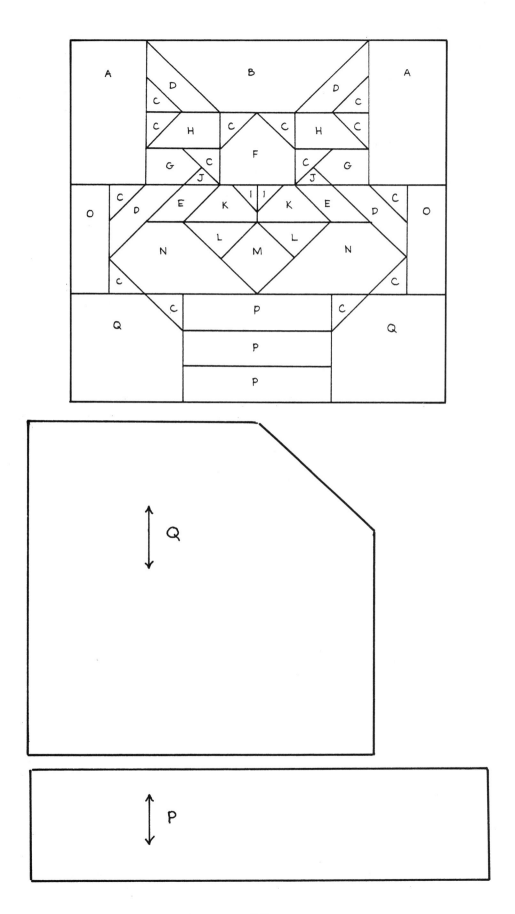

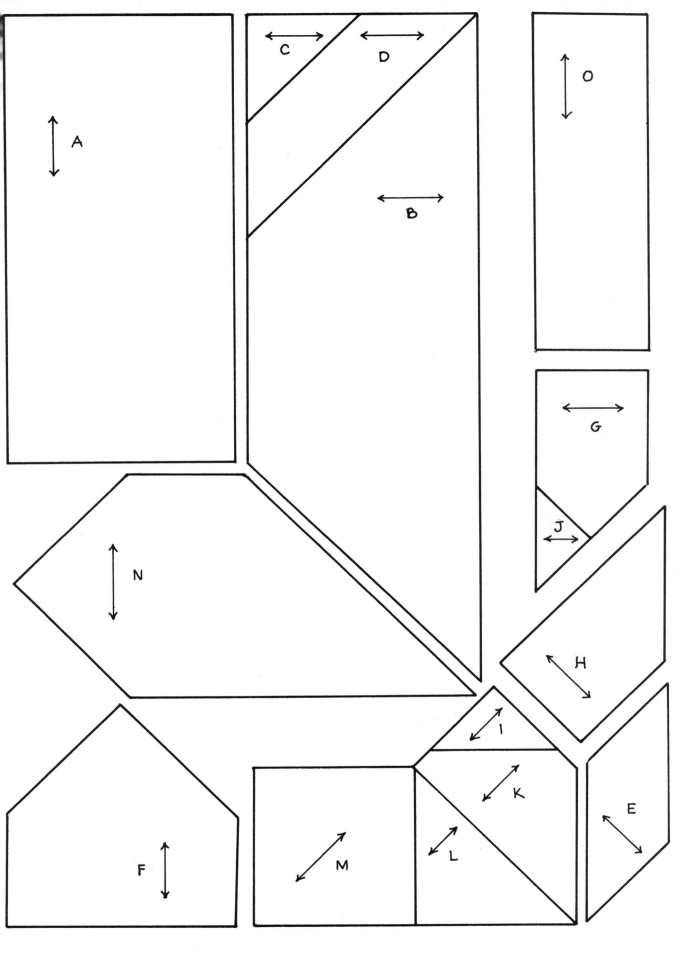

18.
Cat Two

The 12" Cat Two block is moderately easy to do and requires seventeen pattern pieces, A–Q. All pattern pieces are actual size. About ⅓ yard (30.5 cm) of solid fabric, plus a small amount of print, are needed. Whiskers look best when top stitched in shiny white thread before the block is quilted. The Cat Two block is included in The Cat's Meow quilt project, shown in color on page 117.

Assembling the Block

1. Cut all of the necessary pattern pieces, adding a ¼" seam allowance.

2. Using the illustrations and diagrams as a guide, piece the sections together in rows.

Row 1: Starting at the top, between the A's. D + C and D + C to B.
Row 2: Moving down. C + C to E.
Row 3: Moving down. G; C + C; F; C + C; G. Add A to each side.
Row 4: Top of middle section. H, J; K + I; K + I; J, H.

Row 5: Bottom of middle section. N + N to M; L + O and add on C; L + O and add on C. Add F to each side.
Row 6: Bottom section. Q + C; P + P + P; Q + C.

The block is now complete. The whiskers can be added.

Option

The eyes on this and the other two cat blocks can shine or sparkle if you select fabric that will give that effect.

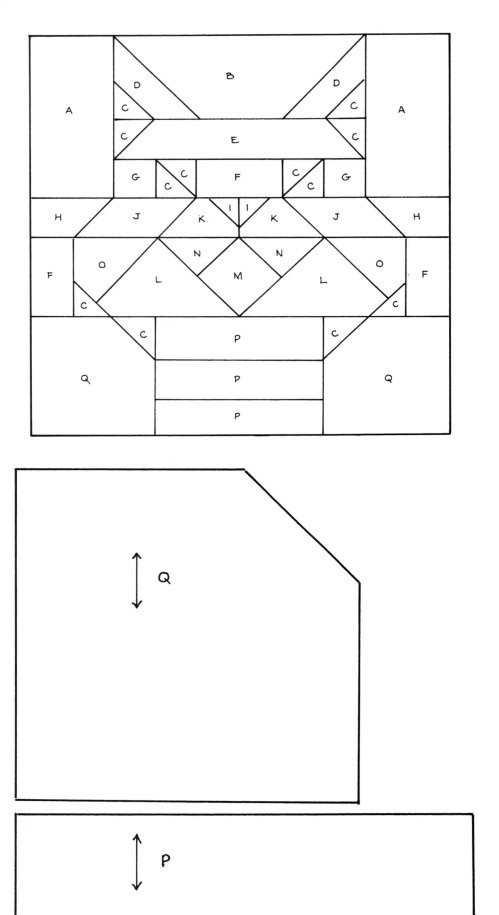

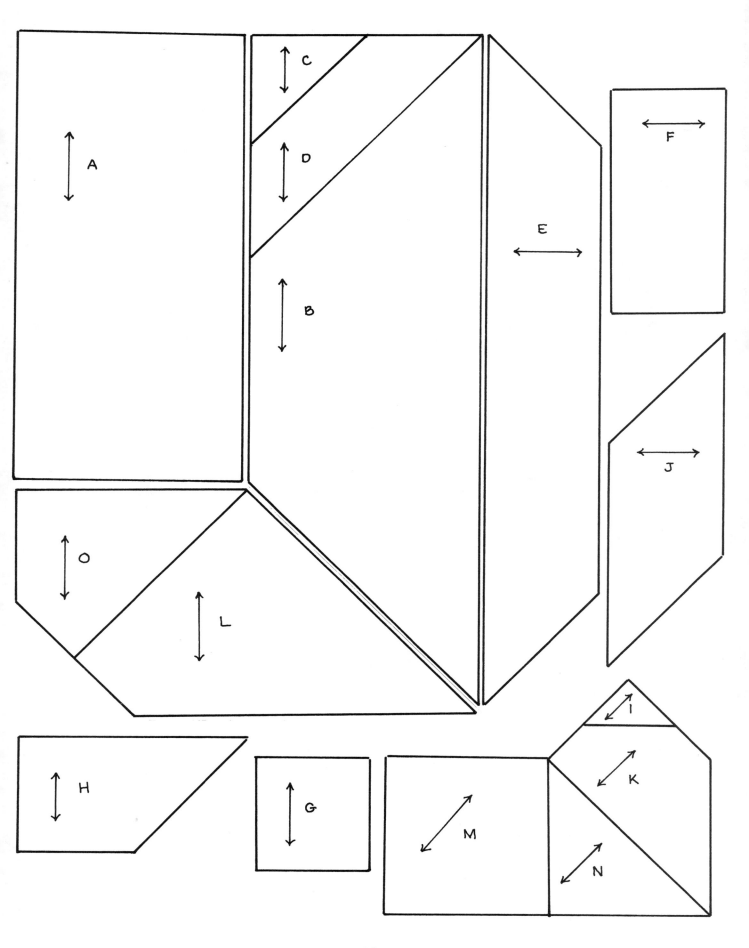

19.
Cat Three

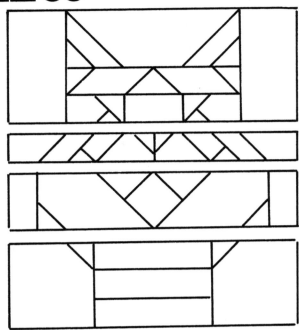

The 12" Cat Three block is moderately easy to do and requires eighteen pattern pieces, A-R. All pattern pieces are actual size. About ⅓ yard (30.6 cm) of solid and print cotton is suggested. Whiskers look best when top stitched, using shiny white thread, before the block is quilted.

Although this cat can be done in all the colors of the previous two, the original was inspired by a Siamese cat; the illustration, therefore, shows those colors. The Cat Three block is included in The Cat's Meow quilt project, shown in color on page 117.

Assembling the Block

1. Cut all of the necessary pattern pieces, adding a ¼" seam allowance.

2. Using the illustrations and diagrams as a guide, sew the sections together in rows.

> *Row 1*: Starting with the top of the top section. D + C and D + C to B.
> *Row 2:* Moving down. C, R, N, R, C.
> *Row 3:* Moving down. G + J to C; F; G + J to C. Add A to each side.
> *Row 4:* Top of middle section. H, E; O +

J; K + I; K + I; O + J; E, H.
> *Row 5:* Bottom of middle section. N + N to M; add L + C to each side. Add F to each side.
> *Row 6:* Bottom section. Q + C; P + P + P; Q + C.

Your block is now complete. Whiskers can now be added.

Option

A collar of jewels is appropriate for a Siamese cat. Already stitched together,

100

jeweled trim can often be purchased by the yard in fabric stores. Attach it to the fabric collar with small stitches from underneath the block where it won't show, and you will have a Siamese cat that is *très élégant!*

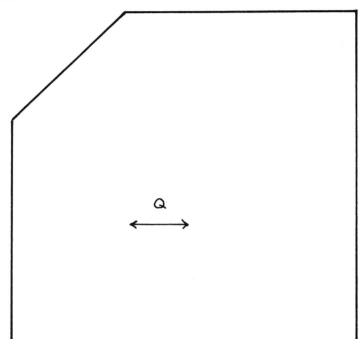

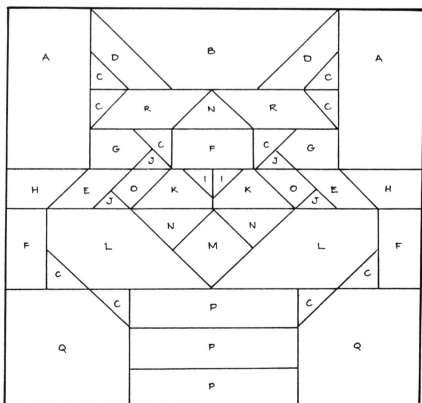

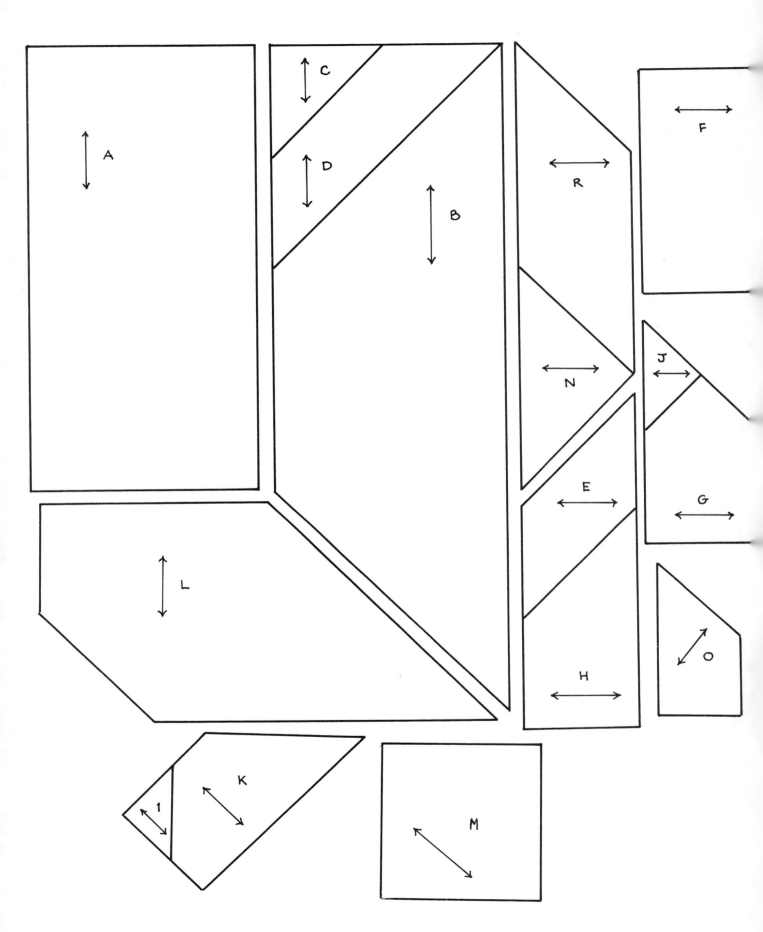

Pieced
Design
Projects

Pieced Design Projects

In this section there are eight projects making use of quilt blocks; these same 12" squares can be used in countless other ways. As you develop your quilting and design skills, various attractive combinations will come to mind.

The first project is a Christmas Sampler which combines three blocks – the Tree, Wreath, and Angel. In Christmas red, holly green, and white, this design will be a welcome addition to holiday decor. The second desisn, the Crab Place Mat, is offered as a useful item for dining. It uses a variation of the Crab block and provides a wonderful opportunity to use color. A Lobster Bib, the third pieced project, is a luxury item. One can be made for each guest attending a very special lobster dinner, a festive occasion in my New England community.

The Town and Country Sampler, the fourth project, is a design using ten of the 12" pieced blocks – Jam Jar, Pineapple, Coffeepot and Cup, Bowl and Pitcher, Blue Jay, Coffee Grinder, Baby Duck, Hen, Bird and Bath, and Teapot – and one double-size 12" by 24" block, the Oil Lamp. This project is country and modern in style at the same time and will be a fine addition to any home.

A variation of the Teapot block is used in the fifth project, a Tea Cozy, which will provide an attractive, practical item for everyday use. The sixth project, Cool Dip, is a bright and cheerful design for a wall quilt. It is made up of the Bird and Bath block and an easy-to-piece flower border. The quilt provides a delightful way to use up lots of scrap fabric.

The seventh design, Country Morning, is a second colorful wall quilt in calico that will blend beautifully in a country-style interior. The design uses only one block – the easy-to-make Bowl and Pitcher. It is another pattern in which scrap fabric can be used.

The Cat's Meow is the eighth and last pieced project, a combination of three delightful 12" blocks – Cats One, Two, and Three. It is designed for the enjoyment of feline fanciers and makes a spectacular gift.

1.
Christmas Sampler

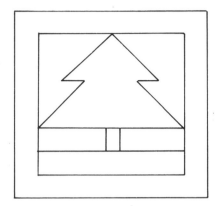
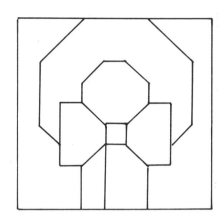

This sampler uses the Tree, Wreath, and Angel blocks. Each is done four times to make a total of twelve blocks. It has 2" sashes, a 3" border on the top and sides, and a 4" border on the bottom. The total size will be about 50" by 65" (125 cm by 162.5 cm), not including the $\frac{1}{4}$" seam allowance. About $1\frac{1}{2}$ yards (1.37 m) of white fabric is needed for the sashes and 2 yards (1.83 m) of holly green for the border. This will allow you to do the border lengths vertically in one piece without cutting and seaming. This is especially nice if you have a flowing design for quilting the border. Some fabric will be left over to use for other projects. The same holly green can be used for the tree and wreath, as shown in the illustration on page 113.

Assembling the Sampler

Place the rows together horizontally, paying special attention to the section on sashes and borders in the Introduction and Instructions. Use the quilt-as-you-go method, and add the sashes, border, and binding, again following the directions in the Introduction and Instructions. In any size, this is a beautiful way to say "Merry Christmas."

2.
Crab Place Mat

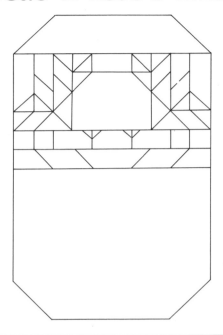

The 12" by 19" place mat is moderately easy to do and requires fifteen pattern pieces, A-O. All pattern pieces are actual size. About ⅓ yard (30.5 cm) of solid and print fabric is needed. This is a variation of the Crab block, and the colors used are similar. You can make your place mat in any colors that you wish. The crab fits nicely to one side, allowing room for dinnerware. The place mat is shown in color on page 114.

Assembling the Place Mat

1. Cut all the necessary pattern pieces, adding a ¼" seam allowance.

2. Using the illustrations and the diagram as a guide, sew the sections together in rows.

Row 1: Starting with the bottom section, left side. J + M; J + K + B; L + K + J; J + K; add on L + L.
Row 2: Middle of bottom section. J + J to G.
Row 3: Bottom. J + J; N; J + J.
Row 4: Right side, bottom left. L + K + J; J + K + B; J + M; K + J, add on L +L.

Row 5: Top section. E, E; F + I; I + I to H; F + I; E, E.
Row 6: B, C, D, C, B.

Add A to the bottom; add O to the top. The top of your place mat is now complete. Use it as a pattern for the batting and backing.

3. Join the three layers together, using the quilt-as-you-go method as described in the sashes and border section of the Introduction and Instructions.

4. Cover the raw edges with continuous bias binding as described in the

continuous bias binding section of the Introduction and Instructions.
The space at the back of the crab can be utilized for sand-color fabric, and the space in front of the crab for water, using colors and textures or prints accordingly.

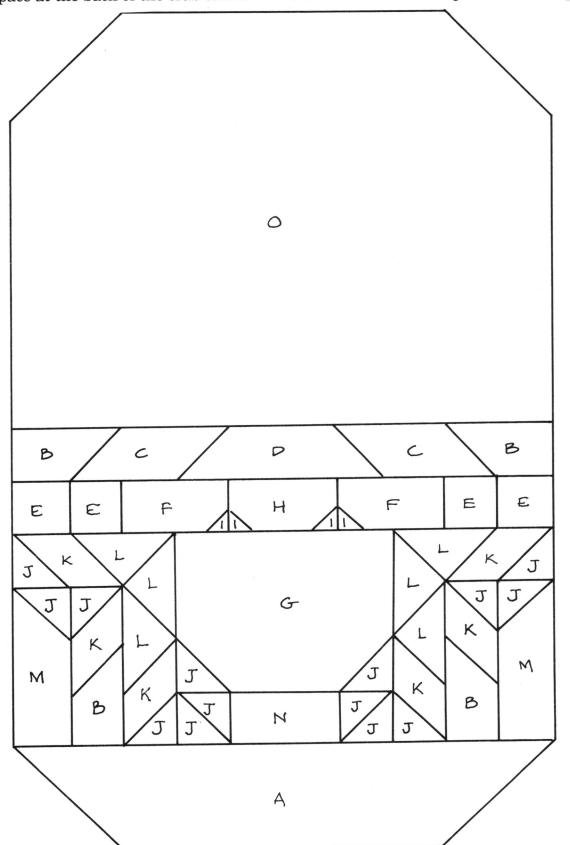

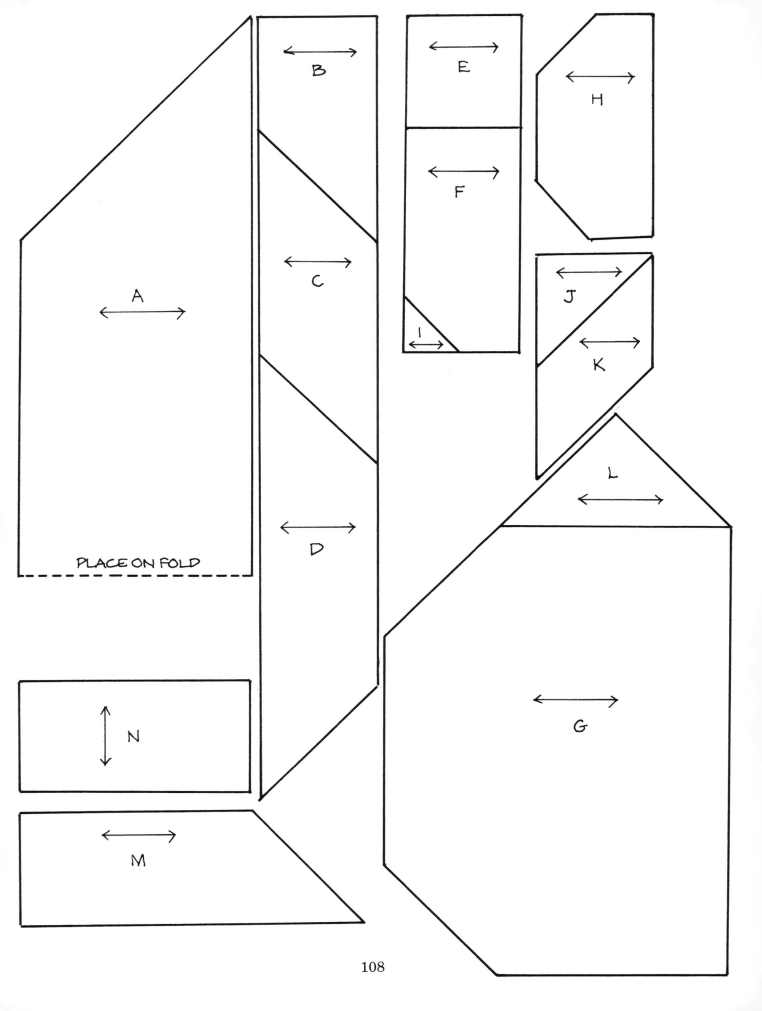

B

E

H

A

C

F

J

I

K

D

L

PLACE ON FOLD

N

G

M

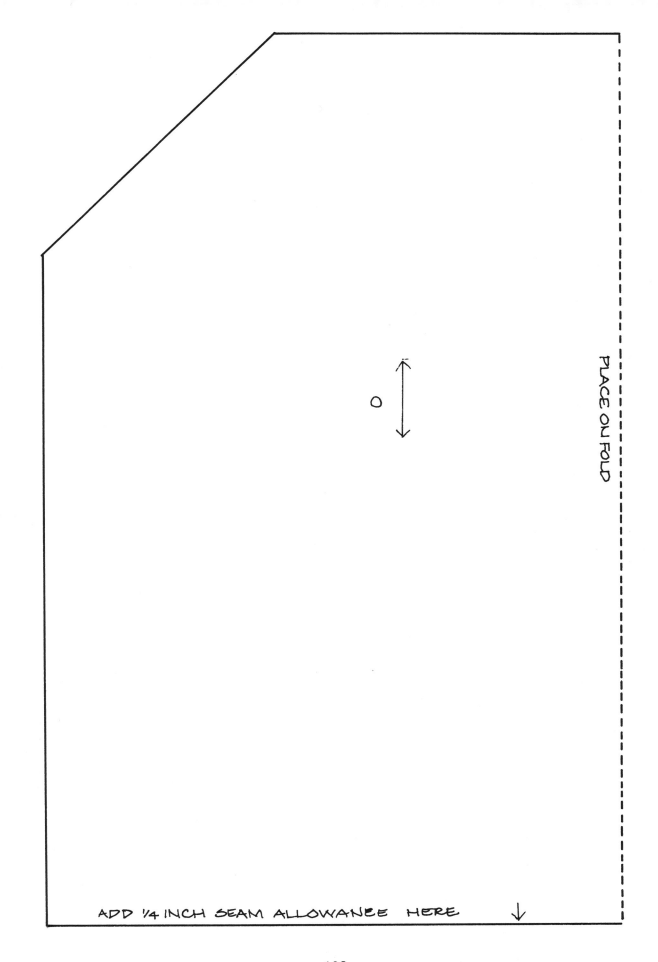

PLACE ON FOLD

ADD ¼ INCH SEAM ALLOWANCE HERE

3.
Lobster Bib

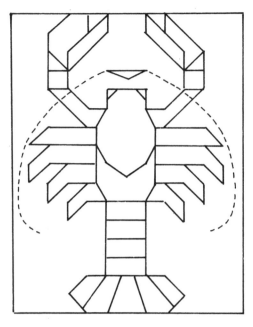

The 12" by 16" Lobster Bib makes use of a variation of the Lobster block and is for the advanced quilter. It has twenty-nine pattern pieces – A-Z and pieces 2, 3, and 4. Many of these pieces are small, making this bib a challenge, but the results will be worth it. All pattern pieces are actual size. Piece one section at a time (arrows on the diagram indicate placement) and then join them. The design is shown in color on page 114.

Assembling the Bib

1. Cut all of the necessary pattern pieces, adding a ¼" seam allowance.

2. Using the illustration and diagram as a guide, sew the sections together in rows.

Row 1: Starting at the bottom. V; C + C + C + C to W; add X and V.
Row 2: Moving up. U, B, U.
Row 3: Moving up. T, C, D, S, D, C, T.
Row 4: Moving up. 2, C, K, N, O, N, K, C, 2.
Row 5: Left side. 3, C, K, R.
Row 6: Moving up. 4, Q.

Row 7: Moving up. 4, Q.
Row 8: Right side. Next to body. R, K, C, 3.
Row 9: Moving up. Q, 4.
Row 10: Moving up. Q, 4.
Row 11: Middle of top section, starting at the bottom. D, N, O, N, D.
Row 12: Moving up. C, K, D; I + I to J; D, K, C.
Row 13: Top section, left side. M, C, E, C.
Row 14: F, G; D + C.
Row 15: Middle of top section. L to H; L to H. Add B.
Row 16: Right side. F, G; C + K; M, C,

Y; add Z.

Row 17: Top, in the middle. D, X, D.

Add A to each side before joining to the lower body section.

The top of the lobster bib is now complete.

3. Use the top as a pattern and cut a back for the bib out of matching fabric. Cut four wide bias strips the width of the dash line on pattern A, adding a ¼" seam allowance at the top edge of A, indicated on the diagram by dash lines. Cut the length of the strips about 12" to fit the average neck size. At the neck, stitch two of the strips to the top of the bib, and two — matching the right sides together — to the back of the bib. This will complete the top and bottom of the bib with the neck strips attached.

4. Use the completed top or bottom of the bib as a pattern to mark the batting. Cut it out and make the "quilt sandwich" the same as for the blocks (see Introduction and Instructions).

5. After the bib is quilted, use continuous bias binding to cover the raw edges. Add Velcro, a button, or snaps on the end of the strips to make it easy to secure around the neck.

Save this, and the other lobster bibs you will make, for a very special lobster dinner.

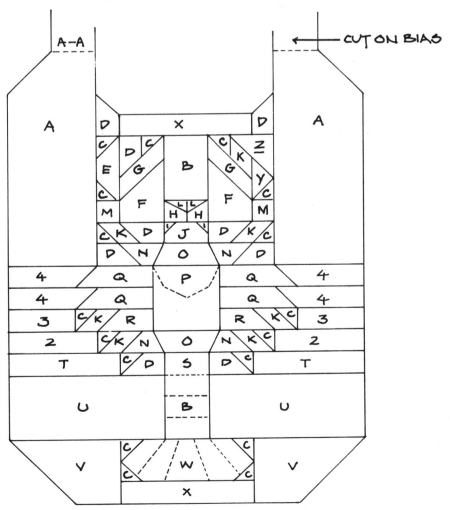

111

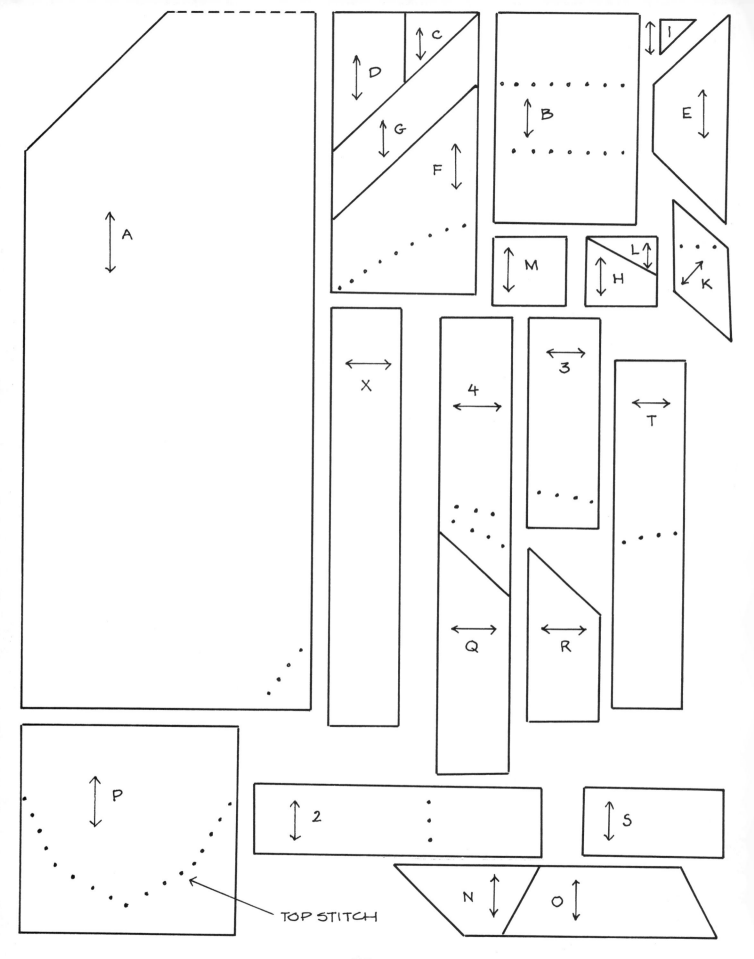

TOP STITCH

Pattern pieces continued on page 121.

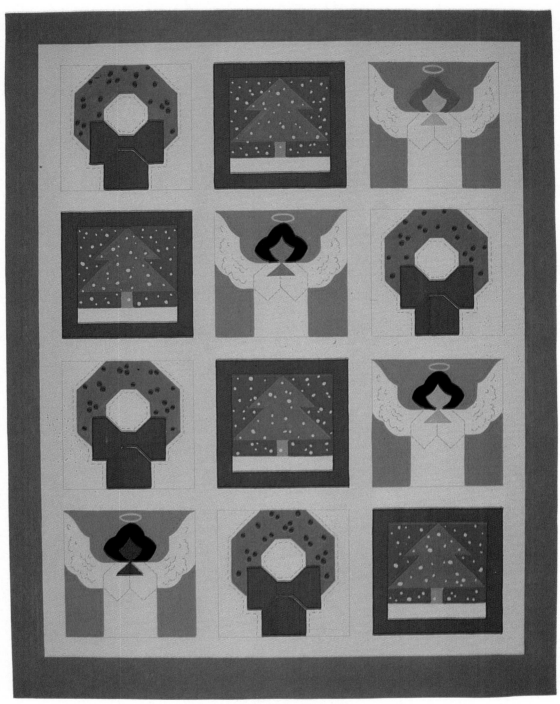

1. Christmas Sampler

2. Crab Placemat

3. Lobster Bib

4. Town and Country Sampler

6. Cool Dip

7. Country Morning

8. The Cat's Meow

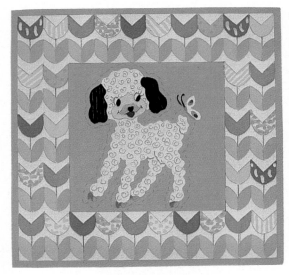

1. Woolykins

3. Lionhearted

118

2. ABCs of Love

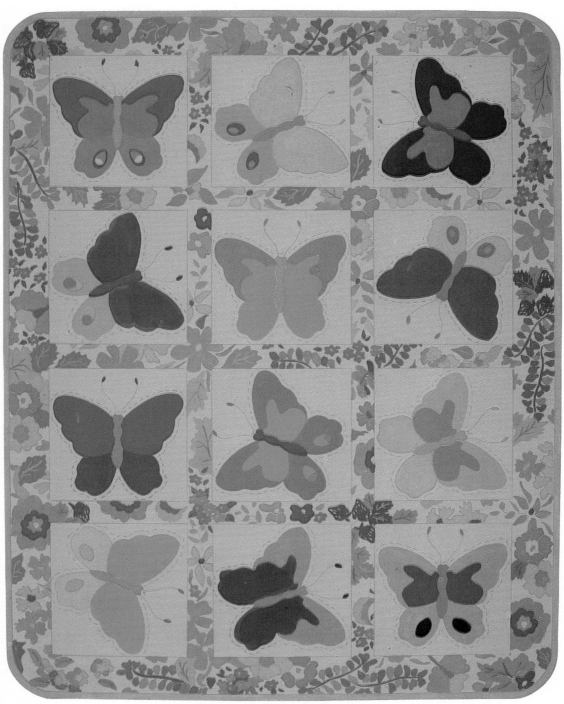

4. Butterflies in My Garden

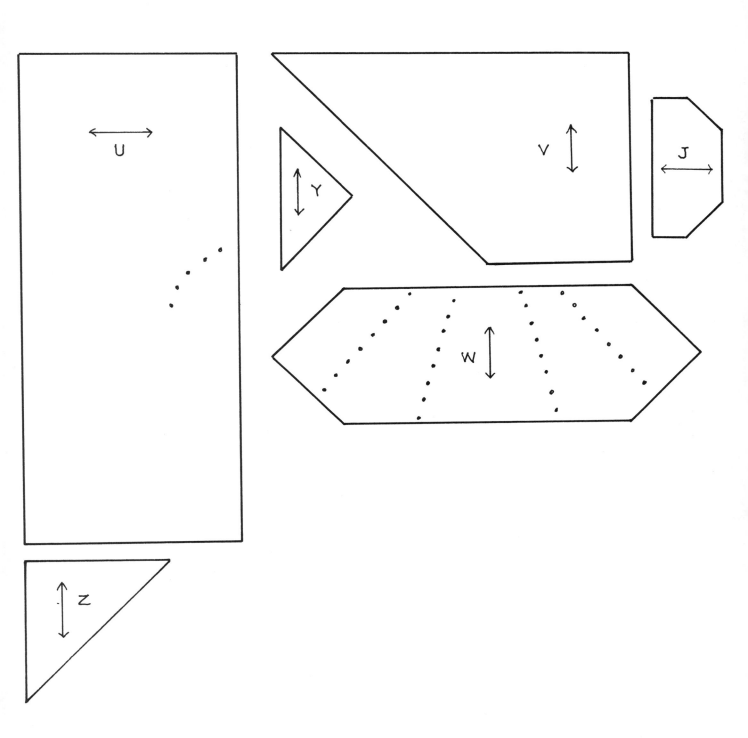

4.
— Town and Country Sampler —

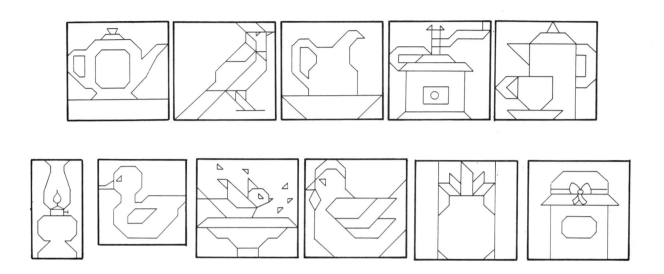

This sampler quilt makes use of the following blocks: Jam Jar, Pineapple, Hen, Bird and Bath, Baby Duck, Oil Lamp, Coffeepot and Cup, Coffee Grinder, Bowl and Pitcher, Blue Jay, and Teapot. Each block is used once to make a total of eleven blocks. Ten of the blocks are the popular 12" size, and one – Oil Lamp – is double size, 12" by 24". Town and Country Sampler, seen in color on page 115, has 2" sashes and a 2" binding, half of which is turned to the back of the quilt. Add a ¼" seam allowance to all measurements. The total size will be about 48" by 62". About 1½ yards (1.37 m) of white fabric for the sashes will allow you to do the length of the sashes without cutting and seaming. You will have some leftover fabric for other projects. About 6¼ yards (5.72 m) of continuous bias binding will also be needed.

Assembling the Sampler

Piece the rows together vertically, paying special attention to the section on sashes and borders in the Introduction and Instructions. Add the binding and blind stitch in place.

If you want to use all 12" blocks, there are several alternative pieced blocks in this book that you can substitute.

5.
Tea Cozy

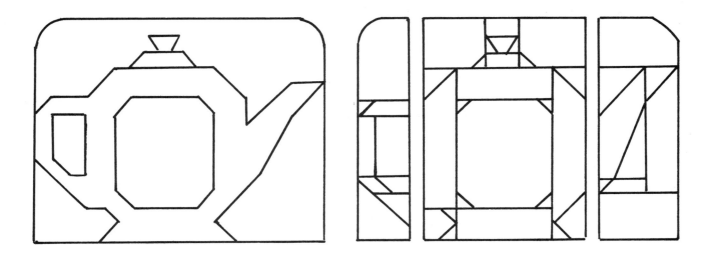

The 9½" by 11½" rounded Tea Cozy uses a variation of the Teapot block. It requires twenty-five pattern pieces, A-Y (including W, the optional tea bag). About ⅓ yard (30.5 cm) of solid and print fabric is needed. All patterns are actual size.

Assembling the Tea Cozy

1. Cut all of the necessary pattern pieces, adding a ¼" seam allowance.

2. Using the diagrams as a guide, sew the sections together in rows.

Row 1: Left side, starting at the bottom. O; U + V + E; T, B; L + C; A.

Row 2: Middle, starting left to right, at the bottom. C + C to P; S, E.

Row 3: Center. C + C + C + C to Q; add on N and N.

Row 4: Right side of center. R + C; M, E.

Row 5: On top. D + C; I + I to H; add G and G; D + C and D + C.

Row 6: Right side, starting at the bottom. A; L + C; X, Y, J; K + E; add on F.

The top of your tea cozy is now complete.

3. Use the top as a pattern to cut the batting and the backing. The backing can be another Teapot pattern, or not, as you wish.

4. Quilt and join the layers, using the quilt-as-you-go method described in the Introduction and Instructions. Use continuous bias binding around the bottom raw edges.

For hanging purposes, add a plastic loop or a matching fabric loop to the top. If you use a fabric loop, attach it at the center point on the top edge as you are joining the front seam to the back.

Option

Another very attractive touch is to use

piping in a matching color on the edge between the front and back. Add it as you do the joining seam (hand baste before stitching.)

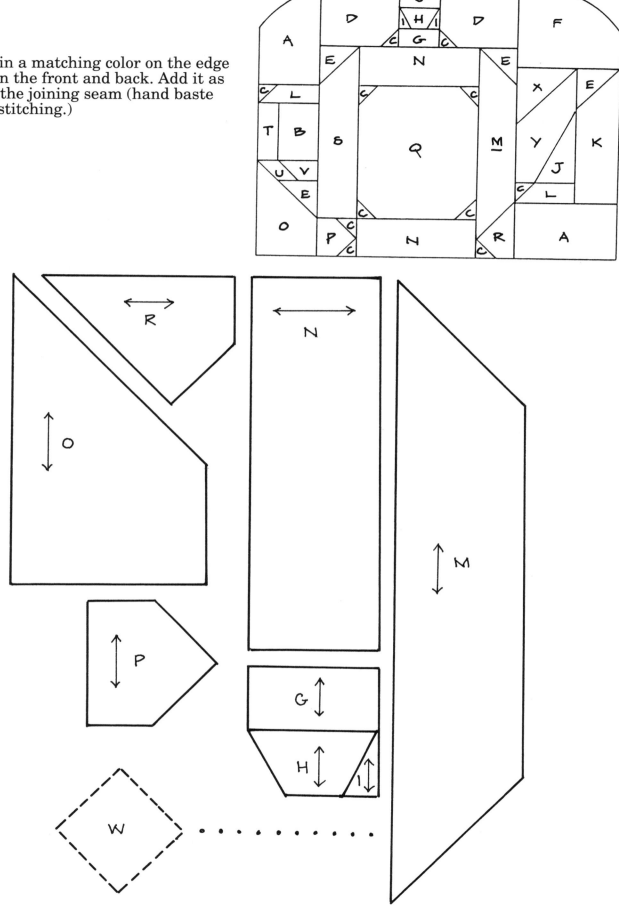

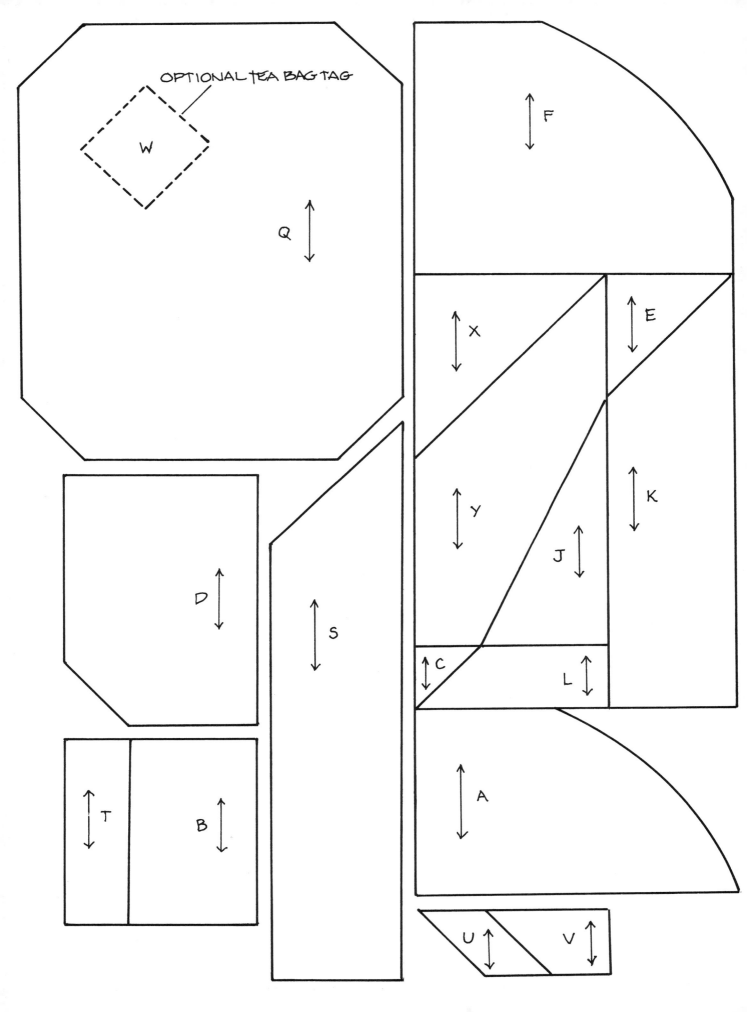

OPTIONAL TEA BAG TAG

W

Q

F

X

E

Y

K

J

D

S

C

L

A

T

B

U

V

6.

Cool Dip

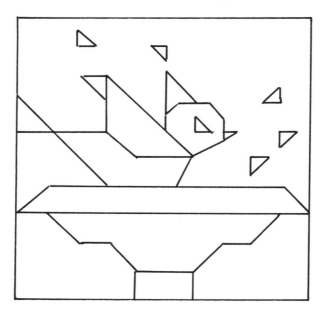

Shown in color on page 116, the 23" by 26" (56.5 cm by 65 cm) Cool Dip wall quilt design is charming, colorful, and easy to make. Use and follow the directions for the Bird and Bath block for the center. The 2½" by 6" (6.4 cm by 15.2 cm) flower pattern for the border requires only three pattern pieces, A-C. A small amount of scrap fabric for each flower is required.

Assembling Cool Dip

The diagram for the flower pattern contains only two rows and is easy to follow.

Row 1: From the bottom. C, B, B, A, C.
Row 2: The same as 1, with the templates reversed.

Make twenty-five more. Add a ¼" seam allowance to all measurements.

Use the color illustration on page 116 as a guide to join the flowers to the block.

Add four on each side first; then add a complete row on top and bottom. The 2" binding (half of which is turned to the back of the quilt) requires about 3 yards (2.74 m) of continuous bias binding.

Cool Dip is a lovely quilt for gift giving. It will make a "big splash" by itself.

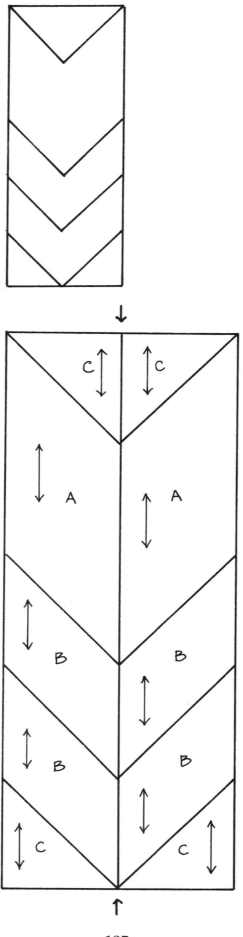

7.
Country Morning

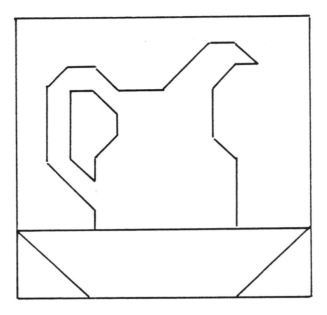

The 44" (111.8 cm) square Country Morning wall quilt design is made up of nine Bowl and Pitcher blocks with 2" sashes and corner blocks. Add a ¼" seam allowance to all measurements, About ⅔ yard (61 cm) of solid-color fabric for the sashes and less than ¼ yard (22.9 cm) of contrasting fabric for the corner blocks are required. The project is illustrated in color on page 116.

Assembling Country Morning

Piece the rows together in any direction, paying special attention to the section on sashes and borders in the Introduction and Instructions. Add a small 1" continuous bias binding to the outside edge, and turn entirely to the back of the quilt. About 5 yards (4.57 m) of bias binding is necessary.

8.
The Cat's Meow

 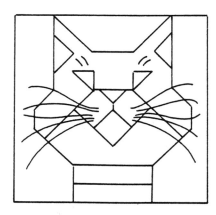 

Shown in color on page 117, the 48" by 62" (3.6 m by 4.69 m) Cat's Meow quilt design is a fabulous quilt project. It is made up of the three cat block designs – Cats One, Two, and Three – in any combination of colors you would like, making a total of twelve cat blocks. Add a ¼" seam allowance to all measurements. You will need about 1½ yards (1.37 m) of white fabric for the sashes and about 6¼ yards (72 m) of 2" continuous bias binding for the outer edge.

Assembling The Cat's Meow

Piece the rows together horizontally, paying special attention to the section on sashes and borders in the Introduction and Instructions. Add the binding and blind stitch the last edge.

Finding just the right fabric for each cat is part of the fun of making The Cat's Meow. Any cat lover will be delighted to have this quilt. Make one for yourself and one for a friend. When this quilt is done, you will almost be able to hear the cats meow!

Appliqué
Design
Blocks

There are three charming blocks to appliqué in this section – a 12" Butterfly, Lion, and Lamb. All are wonderful for making quilts and other useful and practical items. You will find the individual instructions for each block easy to follow. All of the blocks are appliquéd by the two fast and easy machine methods outlined in the Introduction and Instructions. If you are a beginner, I recommend starting with Method Two. The blocks can be used by themselves, with pieced blocks, or with other 12" blocks you might have in your collection.

Color is very important to the look of the finished block. Even though the colors shown are my choices, I encourage you to try many variations of your own; the possibilities are endless. If you have avoided appliqué in the past, this is the time to give it an honest effort. You will love the results!

1.
Butterfly

The 12" Butterfly block is very easy to do, excellent for beginners, and requires only five pattern pieces, A-E, if you top stitch or embroider the antennae. If you wish to appliqué the antennae tips, two additional pattern pieces are needed, F and G. All pattern pieces are actual size. About ⅓ yard (30.5 cm) of solid and print cotton fabric is needed. The Butterfly block is the essential pattern for the Butterflies in My Garden quilt project, illustrated in color on page 120.

Although this pattern is one of the easiest to do, there is plenty of opportunity for color. On the butterfly alone there are three sections, not including the "eye" on the bottom part of the wing (pattern E), that invite color. The eye is optional, but it does give you another area for color. You might like to add it on some butterflies and not on others.

Butterflies are a symbol of fragile beauty and independence, very much like children. As you quilt this block, consider planting a flowering shrub that will attract the real butterflies to your garden. Having seen your beautiful quilt, the children will already know what to look for when the blossoms appear.

Assembling the Block

1. Cut all of the necessary pattern pieces as they are. Do *not* add a seam allowance.

2. Using the illustration and diagram as a guide, place each fabric piece for the butterfly on the 12" block, side by side as

follows:

Start with the body, A; add the wings, B, C, D; the wing "eye," E; and, if you wish, the antennae tips, F and G. Tilt some of the butterflies on an angle.

3. When you are sure the spacing looks good, and you are ready to appliqué, refer to the two machine appliqué methods in the Introduction and Instructions. Using one of the methods, appliqué the butterfly to the block.

Option

If you would like to give a more handmade look to your butterfly, outline by hand, with a running stitch in one strand of embroidery floss, about $1/4$", beyond the image. Beyond that, another $1/4$", you can add a quilting outline. The embroidery thread should be in a color that goes well with your butterfly.

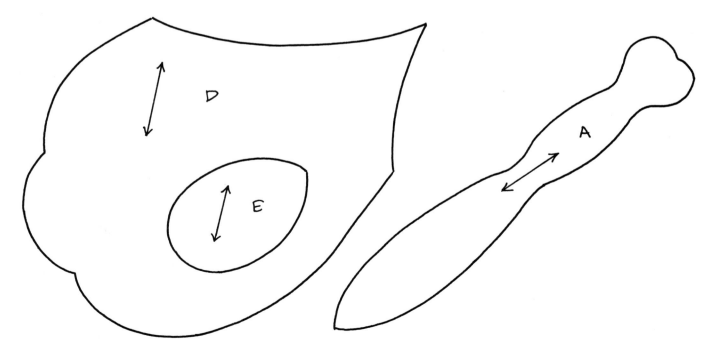

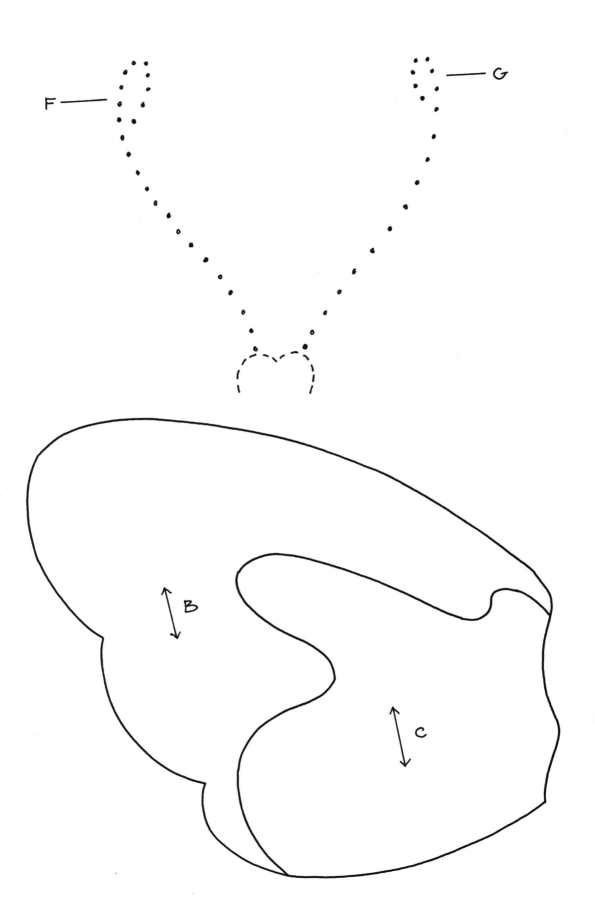

2.
Lion

The 12" Lion block is easy to do, good for begninners, and requires only ten pattern pieces, A-J. All pattern pieces are actual size. About ⅓ yard (30.5 cm) of solid and print cotton fabric is needed. The lion presents a happy, cheerful image, and his mane is the perfect place for a contrasting fabric. The small circles just over his mouth can be painted on with fabric paint, or, if you like to hand embroider, they can be done with French knots. The whiskers look best when top stitched, before the quilt sandwich is made. This majestic lion is shown in color in the Lionhearted quilt project on page 118.

Assembling the Block

1. Cut all of the necessary pattern pieces as they are. Do *not* add a seam allowance.

2. Using the illustration and diagram as a guide, place each fabric piece for the lion on the block, side by side, as follows:

Start with the mane, G; add the face, A; body, H; tail, J + I; ears, B; nose, C; mouth and nose area, F and D; and tongue, E.

3. When you are sure the spacing looks good, and you are ready to appliqué, refer to the two machine appliqué methods in the Introduction and lnstructions. Using one of the methods, appliqué the lion to the block.

Options

The Lion, the Lamb (see page 139), and the three Cats (see pages 94, 97, and 100) can also be used to decorate a child's room. They can be appliquéd to curtains, pillows, and bed skirts to match the delightful quilt you will be making. You can also use them for the walls. Just trace around the templates to get the image; then simply paint them on the wall with latex paint in colors to match the room. They can be painted all around the room at eye level, or all together on one wall, or however you wish. Your room and your creative sense will tell you how to do it.

The Lion and the Lamb, in combination with red and green fabric, will make a beautiful Christmas quilt.

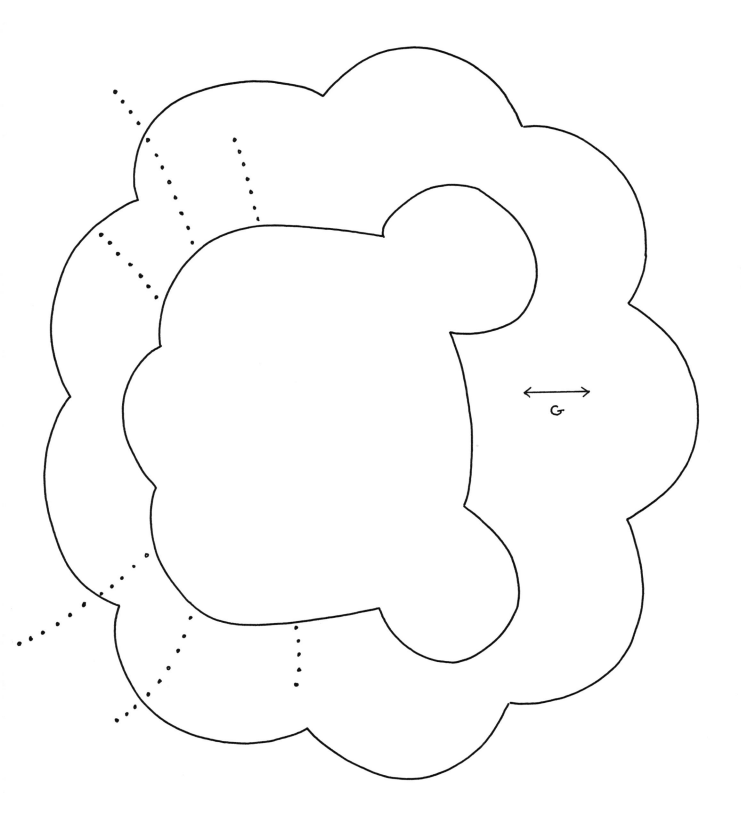

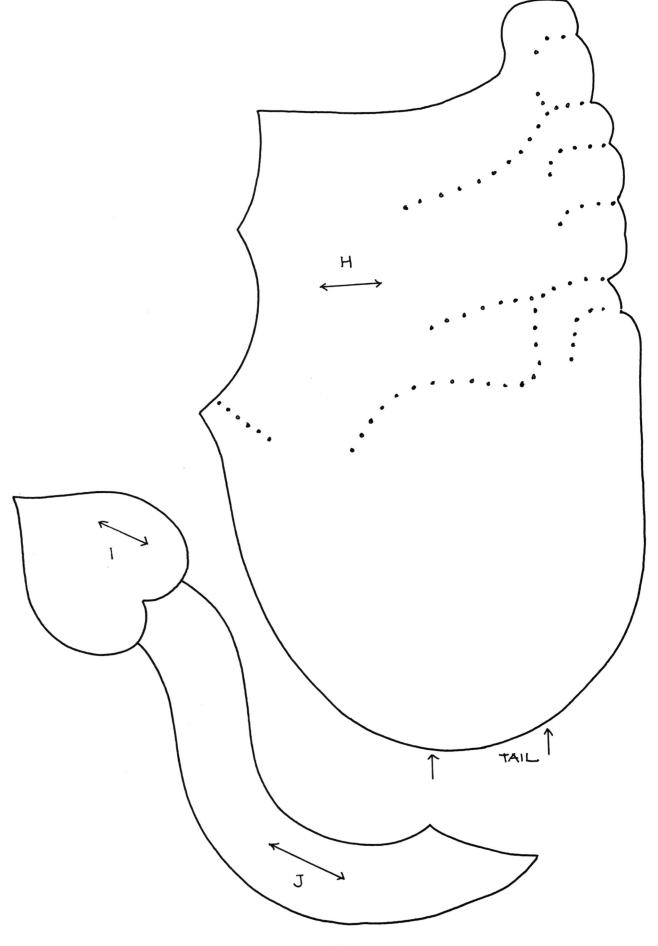

H

I

J

TAIL

3.
Lamb

The 12" Lamb block is moderately easy to do and requires fifteen pattern pieces, A-O. The optional butterfly has six pattern pieces, A-F. All pattern pieces are actual size. About ⅓ yard (30.5 cm) of print and solid cotton fabric is needed. Purchase a rose bow for under the chin. The black ears are quite startling next to all that white, so you can soften the effect by using a black print with a small amount of white in it. I searched for weeks to find just the right print without much success, only to have it practically fall in my lap at a friendship quilt exchange. One of the members of our quilting group gave me a large enough scrap piece from fabric she used in her block after I admired it and mentioned that it would be just right for my lamb. Such kindness is what makes some quilters the very special people that they are. This gentle lamb is included in the Woolykins quilt project illustrated in color on page 118.

Assembling the Block

1. Cut all of the necessary pattern pieces as they are. Do *not* add a seam allowance.

2. Using the illustration and diagram as a guide, place each fabric piece for the lamb on the block as follows:

   Start with the body, J; add on the head, A, G; ears, E, F; eyes, H + I; nose portion, B, C, D; tail, K; and hooves, L, M, N, and O.

3. When you are sure the spacing looks good, and you are ready to appliqué, refer to the two methods of machine appliqué in the Introduction and Instructions. Using one of the methods, appliqué the lamb to the block. Top stitch all lines with dots.

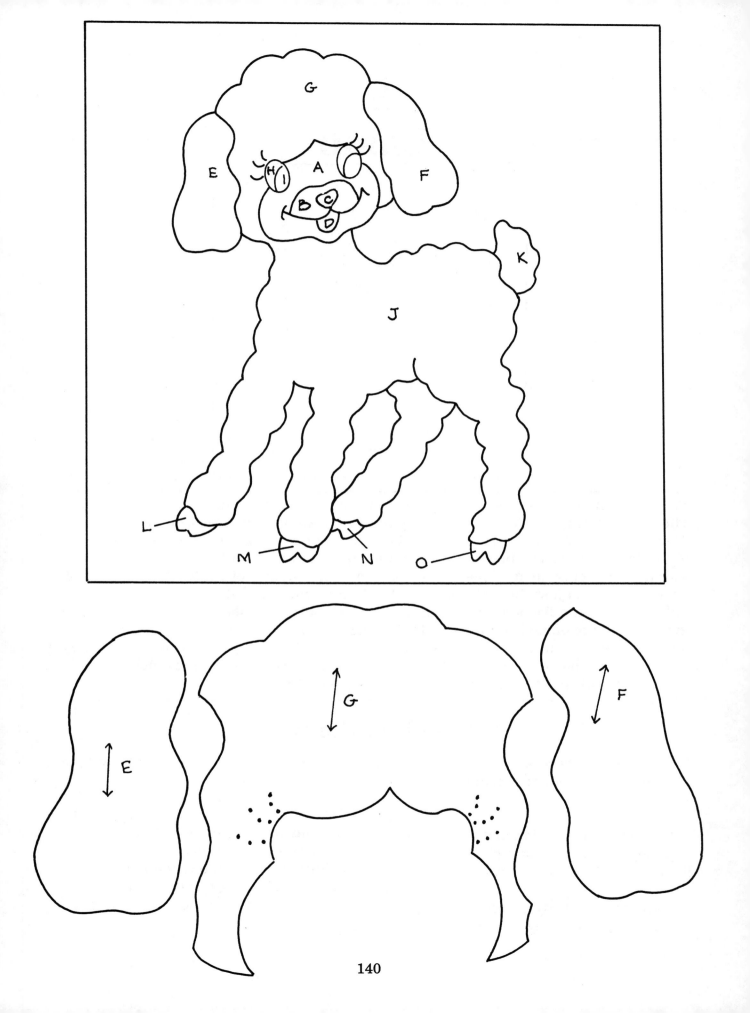

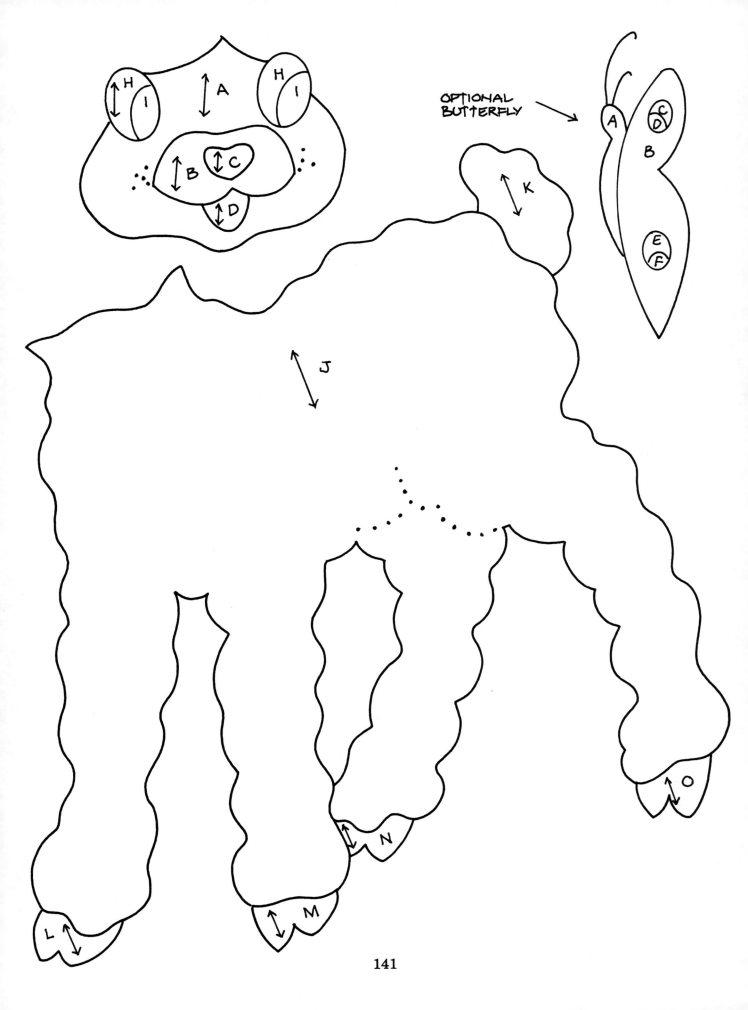

OPTIONAL BUTTERFLY

Appliqué
Design
Projects

You will find four projects in this section for you to enjoy. The first is a wall quilt titled Woolykins. It includes the Lamb block and a flower border. A pattern is included for the border as well as for the small optional butterfly. A lovely and colorful design, it is suited for all children, but will be very special for a baby if worked in pastel colors. The flower border can also be combined with any of the other 12" block designs.

The second project is a baby quilt called ABCs of Love. This quilt design is made up of fifty-four 4" blocks. In solid pastel-color and/or print fabrics, this design will make a perfect baby gift.

Another wall quilt, affectionately known as Lionhearted, makes up the third project. This design uses the Lion block along with hearts and letters. It is perfect for a child born under the sign of Leo. Any of the other 12" blocks in this book can be combined with hearts and letters so long as the letters will fit into the five spaces on top and/or on bottom.

The fourth project, one of the most beautiful, is called Butterflies in My Garden and uses only *one* 12" butterfly pattern. The sashes and border are designed with a flower print. The color potential of this quilt design is one of its strengths.

1.
Woolykins

This delightful wall quilt uses the 12" appliqué Lamb block and a pieced flower border. You have a choice of two flower patterns, one with straight edges and one with curved edges. If you are a beginner, the flower pattern with all straight edges will be easier. The experienced quilter will find the few curved edges on the other flower pattern easier to piece by hand than by machine. The flower size is 2" by 4" (5.1 cm by 10.2 cm), perfect for using lots of scrap fabric. You will need about 2 ⅓ yards (2.13 m) of 2" bias binding. The total wall quilt size is approximately 20" (50.8 cm) square and is shown in color on page 118.

Assembling the Flower

Straight Edges

1. Cut all the necessary pattern pieces, adding a ¼" seam allowance.

2. Using the illustration and diagram as a guide, piece the sections together in rows.

> *Row 1:* Starting at the top, and moving down. B, A, B.
> *Row 2:* B, A, B.
> *Row 3:* B, A, B.
> *Row 4:* B, A, B.

Your straight-edged flower is now complete. Make thirty-one more.

Curved Edges

1. Cut all of the necessary pattern pieces, adding a ¼" seam allowance.
2. Using the illustration and diagram as a guide, piece the sections together in rows.

> *Row 1:* B, A, B.
> *Row 2:* C + C to D (do by hand).
> *Row 3:* F + F to E (do by hand).

144

Row 4: C + C to D (do by hand).

The curved flower block is now complete. Make thirty-one more.

3. Add the flowers to each side of the Lamb block first. Then add the complete flower rows on top and bottom. Add binding.

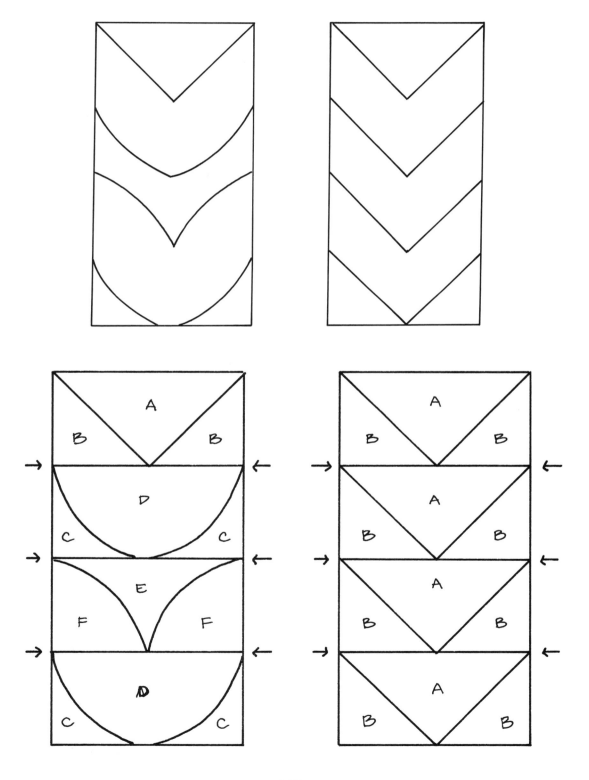

2.

The ABCs of Love

This colorful baby quilt design project uses one heart pattern and all of the twenty-six letters of the alphabet appliquéd to fifty-four 4" blocks. The diagram provides a guide for placement of the hearts and letters. The illustration on page 119 shows solid colors, but pastel-color prints and/or solid-color fabric will look beautiful also. This is a perfect scrap quilt design.

Appliqué Method Two, using fusible transfer web (see Introduction and Instructions), is advised for this project. Because the 4" blocks are so small, they are a pleasure to work with on the sewing machine. The border is 3" wide on all sides. The total size will be about 30" by 42". You will need a little more than 4 yards (3.66 m) of 2" binding of a color to match the border.

Assembling the Blocks

1. Cut all of the necessary pattern pieces as they are; do *not* add a seam allowance.

2. Appliqué the hearts and letters to the blocks, using Method Two.

3. Using the illustration and diagram as a guide, sew the blocks together horizontally in rows.

Row 1: Starting from the top, moving down. One heart; A, B, C; two hearts.
Row 2: D; two hearts; E, F; one heart.
Row 3: G; one heart; H; two hearts; I.
Row 4: J, K; two hearts; L; one heart.
Row 5: One heart; M; one heart; N; one heart; O.
Row 6: P; one heart; Q; one heart; R; one heart.

Row 7: One heart; S; one heart; T; one
heart; U.

Row 8: V; three hearts; W; one heart.
Row 9: two hearts; X, Y; one heart; Z

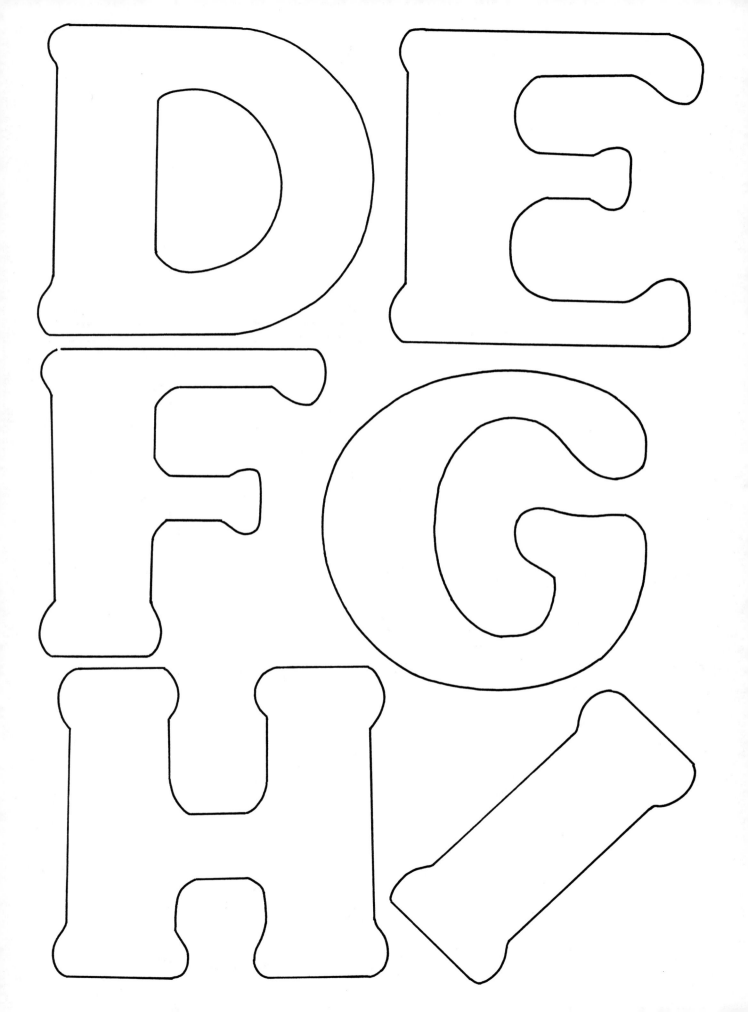

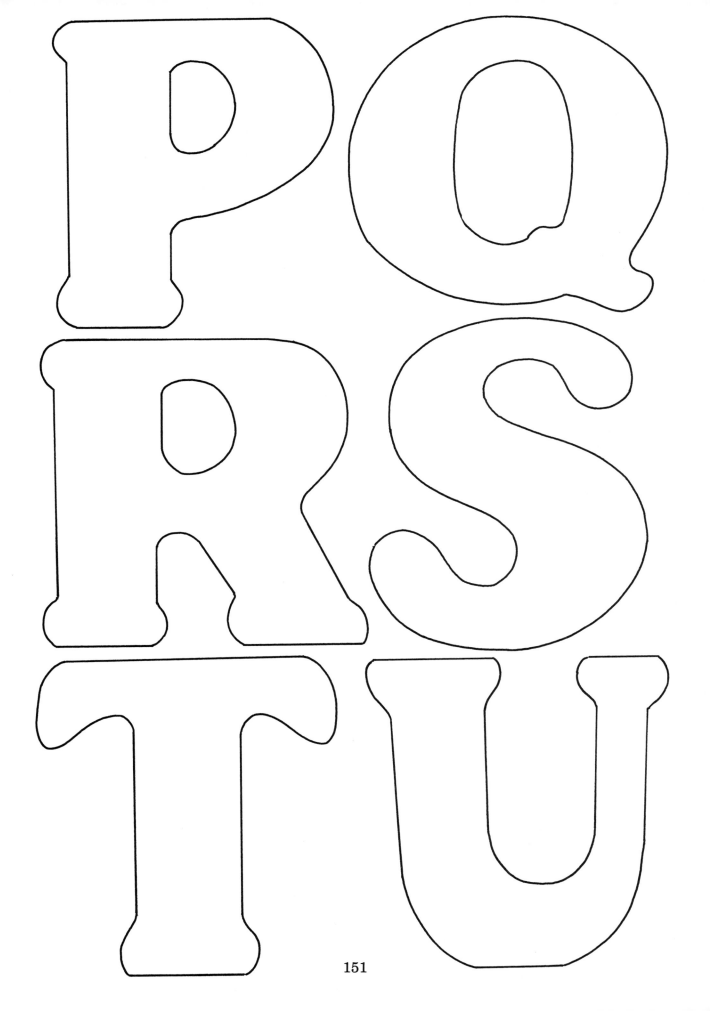

3.
Lionhearted

This bright and cheerful wall quilt makes use of the Lion block; the letters L, I, O, N (from the letters of the alphabet in the ABCs of Love project); and twelve hearts (from the ABCs of Love) in a print that matches the lion's mane. Appliqué, using Method Two. If you wish to use the print fabric line under the lion and over the letters, as shown in the color illustration on page 118, cut a 1½" (including seam allowance) piece of print fabric on the straight of the grain. Add it to the bottom of the Lion block and one Heart block after you have removed 1" from the bottom of both to make up the difference.

The total size will be about 20" (50.8 cm) square before binding. You will need about 2⅓ yards of 2" binding (the same fabric as the lion's mane).

Assembling the Blocks

Join the six hearts to the sides of the Lion block, and then add the two rows of hearts on top and bottom. Bind the outside edge of the quilt, turning half of the bias binding to the back of the quilt. Blind stitch in place.

Option

In addition to the Lion, other little friends can be used in a small wall quilt like this one. Here is a wonderful opportunity to combine pieced and appliqué blocks in the same quilt. The Cat, Duck, Hen, Crab, and Bird have the right number of letters in their names to fit in the five available spaces. Any combination will make a wonderful quilt.

4.
—— Butterflies in My Garden ——

Only *one* easy-to-do appliqué pattern – the Butterfly – is required to make this outstandingly beautiful quilt. One flowered print cotton fabric is suggested for the sashes and the border. Twelve solid-color butterflies combine in a variety of positions on the 12" blocks for this design. The project is illustrated in color on page 120.

Butterflies in My Garden has 2" sashes and a 4" border that is rounded off at the corners. I use a dinner plate appropriate to the size of the border to do this. The total size of the quilt will be about 50" by 64" (127 cm by 162 cm). The continuous bias binding is 2" wide, half of which is turned to the back of the quilt. You will need about 6⅓ yards of binding.

Assembling the Blocks

Join the blocks horizontally, using the graph paper diagram in the Introduction and Instructions as a guide.

Throughout this book I have suggested many-ways to use a wide variety of quilt block designs. I hope you will think of them as mere starting points and create many more desisns of your own. Have a quilterrific time!

Metric Equivalents

INCHES TO MILLIMETRES AND CENTIMETRES

MM—millimetres   CM—centimetres

Inches	MM	CM	Inches	CM	Inches	CM
⅛	3	0.3	9	22.9	30	76.2
¼	6	0.6	10	25.4	31	78.7
⅜	10	1.0	11	27.9	32	81.3
½	13	1.3	12	30.5	33	83.8
⅝	16	1.6	13	33.0	34	86.4
¾	19	1.9	14	35.6	35	88.9
⅞	22	2.2	15	38.1	36	91.4
1	25	2.5	16	40.6	37	94.0
1¼	32	3.2	17	43.2	38	96.5
1½	38	3.8	18	45.7	39	99.1
1¾	44	4.4	19	48.3	40	101.6
2	51	5.1	20	50.8	41	104.1
2½	64	6.4	21	53.3	42	106.7
2	76	7.6	22	55.9	43	109.2
3½	89	8.9	23	58.4	44	111.8
4	102	10.2	24	61.0	45	114.3
4½	114	11.4	25	63.5	46	116.8
5	127	12.7	26	66.0	47	119.4
6	152	15.2	27	68.6	48	121.9
7	178	17.8	28	71.1	49	124.5
8	203	20.3	29	73.7	50	127.0

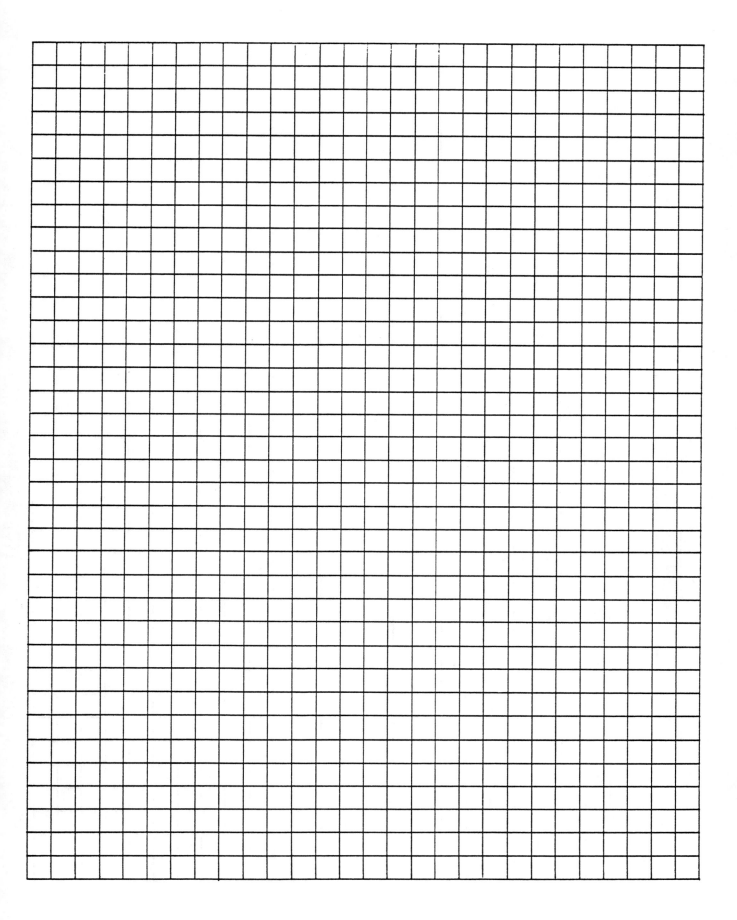

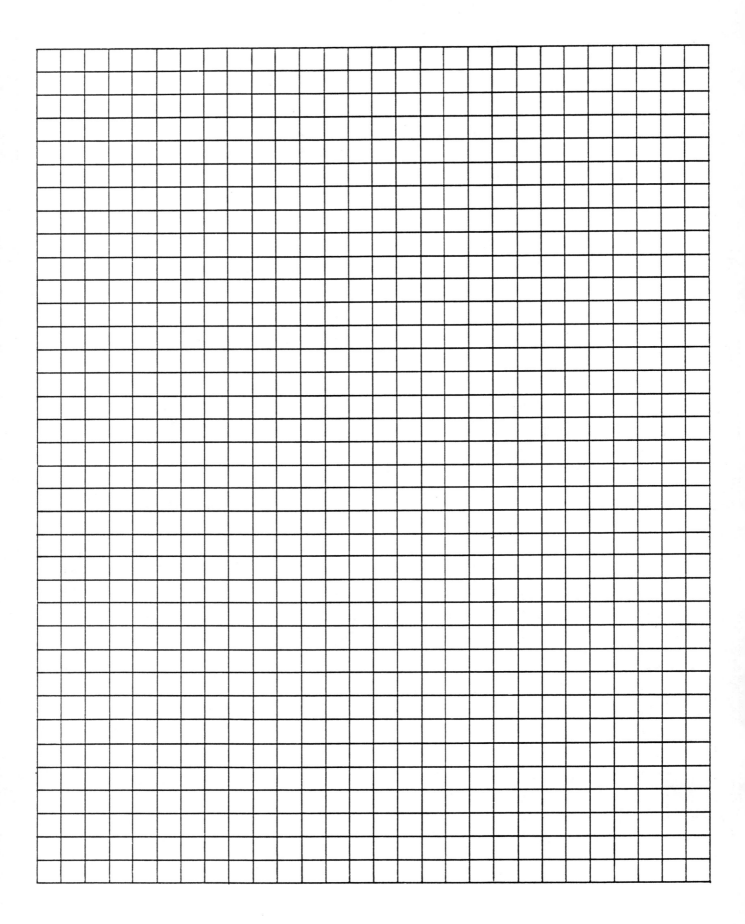

Index